MW01269029

MARIJUANA

BUSINESS

2021

THE LEGAL CANNABIS INDUSTRY IN THE U.S. AND GLOBALLY

OBJECTIVE MARKET-DRIVEN COVERAGE OF GLOBAL CANNABIS INDUSTRY TRENDS AND OPPORTUNITIES

By Elia Friedenthal

Legal & Disclaimer

CONTENTS

CHAPTER 11: Opening A Dispensary 103

INTRODUCTION

With legalization in Canada and many US states, and with the spread of CBD products like wildfire around the world, the cannabis market has hit stellar numbers this year.

The passion for hemp is gaining momentum globally and, according to statistics, the numbers will continue to rise undeterred.

In fact, according to CNN, in 2019 the cannabis market earned about 15 billion dollars and is destined to reach even higher peaks in the years to come.

Over the past two years, CBD products have mushroomed thanks to the advent of legalization in Canada and the increasingly lax laws enacted in several US states. And with the FDA (US Food and Drug Administration) currently planning a CBD-based epilepsy drug, and the government working to regulate over-the-counter CBD products, the market is expected to expand exponentially.

"The decisions made at the federal level put pharmacies and generic retailers into the market for CBD products in all 50 US states, which has greatly improved the projections on annual revenue," says Arcview CEO Troy Dayton, on CNN.

For the first time, in 2019, Arcview included a section called "Total Cannabinoid Market" in the state's annual sales report, including everything from pharmacy, to dispensary, to online sales.

If the current trend continues, it is estimated that by 2024 the cannabis market will reach $44 billion, of which about half in CBD products, a number that surpasses previous statistics by almost $5 billion.

Only time will reveal whether these forecasts will materialize or not, but with legalization in the US continuing to expand and with Canada preparing for a major supply hike, we expect nothing less than a massive surge in sales of legal cannabis.

As of 2019, legal cannabis has created 211,000 full-time jobs in America.

How many jobs are there in the legal cannabis industry? It's a common question, and one the government refuses to answer. Because cannabis remains federally illegal, employment data agencies such as the Bureau of Labor Statistics ignore all industry-related jobs. It's a shame, because one of the most dramatic job booms in recent history is missing. Over the past three months, Leafly 's data team, which works in partnership with Whitney Economics, has been moving from state to state to calculate the total number of direct full-time jobs in the state cannabis legal sector.

There are now more than 211,000 cannabis jobs in the United States. More than 64,000 of these jobs were added in 2018. Legal cannabis is currently the largest job creation machine in America. The strength of the cannabis business increased by 21% in 2017. It gained another 44% in 2018. 20% of the market's growth was in 2019. This represents a growth of 110% in cannabis jobs in just three years.

The Bureau of Labor Statistics recently compiled a list of industries with the fastest growing employment data. Opportunities for home health aides are expected to grow by 47%. Openings for wind turbine technicians are expected to increase by 96%. The need for solar PV installers is expected to grow by 105%. Such gains are expected to occur over the course of 10 years.

Some states that have seen adult cannabis legalization for some time - Colorado and Washington opened their stores in 2014 - are now seeing the growth of jobs around this industry. Meanwhile, new legal states, such as Florida (medical) and Nevada (adult use), are experiencing booms in cannabis work with jaw-dropping earnings:

Florida increased its cannabis use by 703% in 2018, adding over 9,000 full-time jobs.

Nevada added over 7,500 jobs in the same year.

Pennsylvania finished 2017 with around 90 cannabis jobs. It finished 2018 with almost 3,900.

New York increased its cannabis use by 278%, ending 2018 with over 5,000 jobs.

California, Massachusetts, Oklahoma, Florida and Arkansas are looking for talent and they need it now. Cannabis intake in California remained relatively flat in 2018 due to the disruption caused by moving from an unregulated medical system to regulated and licensed markets for medical and adult use. In rough numbers, this means that 10,261 jobs with good salaries, benefits and advancement opportunities are waiting to be filled.

In Massachusetts, the adult state market is just getting started. We expect to add over 9,500 jobs over the next 12 months. Florida is expected to add over 5,000 jobs, bringing the state's total cannabis employment to around 15,000. Oklahoma is the Wild West of cannabis right now. A year ago there were zero cannabis jobs. Now there are 2,107. In a year's time, we expect there will be 4,407. Arkansas has just started its medical marijuana program, but there is room for growth: from 135 jobs to 960 jobs by the end of the year.

Although Europe followed the European Law 242/2016, cultivation and then trade in cannabis derivatives with low THC content was regulated.

The hemp market is not just a trend of the moment, but a business destined to grow in various fields: from recreation, to medicine, to the world of food and cosmetics, the fields of application are numerous.

This has led to the birth of a new economic sector made up of different parts of the supply chain.

It starts with farms that have seen their earning potential increase, then moves on to wholesalers and intermediaries to get to retailers.

If at the end of 2017 there were a few dozen stores throughout Italy, today in 2019 we have reached almost 1000 scattered throughout the peninsula.

A number destined to grow because more and more people will overcome stereotypes and get closer to the cannabis plant.

Those who want to invest therefore have different strategies: you can open a farm dedicated to the cultivation of hemp, become an intermediary, or open a light cannabis shop.

The light cannabis market is in full evolution, if you are a fan and a connoisseur of this plant, you can use your knowledge to also become a successful entrepreneur.

CHAPTER 1: A LITTLE HISTORY OF MARIJUANA

CANNABIS HAS ITS ORIGINS IN ASIA

At some point in history, the cannabis plant started growing in the wilderness. It is possible that it first grew in the areas of passage of hunter-gatherers, rich in nutrients. The farthest point in time that we can confirm the presence of cannabis is roughly 11-12,000 years ago. It would appear that the plant first grew in the mountainous areas of Central Asia, particularly Mongolia and southern Siberia. Humans began to cultivate two different varieties, using them for various purposes. The "Cannabis sativa" plant offered humans a unique psychoactive high. The one classified as "Cannabis sativa L.", however, is the common hemp, a non-psychoactive plant used industrially to produce oil, rope, paper and other materials.

It is difficult to pinpoint the exact moment when humans discovered how to use psychoactive plants. At some point, someone will have decided to smoke some cannabis, to see what happened. Had it not been for this pioneering spirit, perhaps the amazing properties of these two plants would have remained unknown to mankind. Later, two other psychoactive cannabis strains were discovered: Cannabis indica, with a physical and comfortable high, and Cannabis ruderalis, with softer highs and a shorter stature. But to analyze in detail the characteristics of each variety, we must first understand how the plant spread from the mountains of Central Asia to the rest of the world.

GANJA SPREADS AMONG CIVILIZATIONS

About ten thousand years have passed since the discovery of cannabis in Central Asia. During this time, the world expands and the seeds propagate. The first written document attesting to the use of cannabis concerns the Emperor of China Shen Neng in 2737 BC

According to some findings, cannabis may have been used by humans as a traditional remedy for several thousand years. In 2,000 BC, China, Japan, India, the Middle East, Russia and Eastern Europe cultivated the plant for only two purposes: psychoactive cannabis and hemp fiber. Between 2,000 and 1,400 BC the Vedas were written. These are sacred texts of one of the oldest religions in the world, Hinduism. In Atharva Veda, cannabis is mentioned. Some followers of Hinduism drink a cannabis-flavored milk, called bhang, in honor of the god Shiva. In some traditions, Shiva is depicted eating cannabis. According to others, her tears irrigated the Earth, and the cannabis plant flourished there.

HIGHLIGHTS OF THE EARLY HISTORY OF CANNABIS

In 1,550 BC, the Ebers Papyrus of ancient Egypt described the use of cannabis for therapeutic purposes. Over the next thousand years, other cultures acquired this knowledge. Around the 5th century BC, in ancient Greece, Herodotus mentioned cannabis. During his trip to the Middle East, he illustrated the cannabis-infused Turkish bath in which the Scythians participated. Herodotus saw that the

Scythians became euphoric and more sociable after breathing in the steam from the bathroom. In 100 BC, the Chinese began to document the psychoactive impacts of cannabis.

During the next millennium, Islamic expansion spread cannabis to North Africa. In the following years, cannabis spread to East Africa and Europe. The propagation of the plant was favored by trade with the Arab world, and by the wide range of applications associated with cannabis and hemp. The hemp rope was solid and strong, suitable for Europeans' long journeys across the seas. When Europeans began colonizing other parts of the world, they brought hemp with them, encouraging its cultivation. An almost extraordinary fact, considering that today the West applies repressive laws against cannabis.

MARIJUANA SPREADS INTO THE COLONIES

As empires gained wealth and enslaved colonized peoples, their fortunes began to consolidate. The more the invasion expanded, the more distant parts of the world connected with each other. In addition to the terrible legacy of colonialism, this link between continents became more solid through the slave trade, and later, by contract servitude. The Indian diaspora was the result of the occupation of India by the British Empire. Workers were sent from India to South Africa or Jamaica. Many carried cannabis with them, and spread it among local populations.

The Africans of the southern regions already knew the plant from 1400 BC For the Jamaicans, however, the introduction of cannabis was a real marvel. Their term " ganja " derives from a Hindu word which in turn derives from the Sanskrit " ganjika ". The Jamaicans ended up developing their own religious tradition which included cannabis. The Rastafarian religion emerged in the 20th century, and included cannabis as a sacrament in contemplative ceremonies. In modern Western culture, Rastafarian iconography is widely associated with cannabis.

This past century has been quite dramatic for cannabis. The United States is a comprehensive example of what nearly all nations experienced during the 20th century.

CANNABIS ARRIVES IN THE UNITED STATES

The British Empire banned the production of cannabis and hemp in Jamaica in 1913, and in South Africa in 1922. In fact, cannabis was beginning to be considered dangerous. The International Opium Convention of 1925 strictly prohibited the export of "Indian hemp" to countries that banned cannabis. Over the years, an increasing number of international laws reduced the production of cannabis to the bone. In 1920, the United States unsuccessfully attempted to ban alcohol consumption. Eventually they retraced their steps, but continued to press what they called "marijuana".

Some revelations about White House policies, particularly under the direction of President Richard Nixon, show that cannabis was targeted for political reasons.

Cannabis use was associated with ethnic minorities and the countercultural movement, so it was easy to arrest those who belonged to these groups accusing them of drug-related offenses. Despite the painful consequences of the War on Drugs, American growers continued to develop the plant, especially in the more tolerant and culturally open West Coast area. Cannabis was welcome here, but soon the whole United States would rebel against the criminalization of marijuana.

MARIJUANA MOVES TOWARDS LEGALIZATION

Cannabis was first introduced to the United States from the Atlantic Ocean. Today, American growers offer the world some of the finest varieties. In turn, the world has encouraged America to be more persistent in its fight against legalization.

The Netherlands also became famous for their flexibility towards international drug laws. During the 1970s, the state instructed the police to ignore coffeeshops and their cannabis sales, as long as they followed certain guidelines. This caused a coffeeshop boom in Amsterdam and other Dutch cities. Dutch society did not crumble after giving people a space in which to purchase a substance used for millennia by all of humanity. In fact, the nation has made significant improvements, managing more effectively, drug use by the population.

Various countries have started experimenting with more liberal and lax cannabis laws. In the 2000s, Spanish cannabis clubs were able to take advantage of a loophole in European legislation. In these premises, reserved exclusively for members of legal age, only the consumption and cultivation of cannabis plants for personal and non-profit use was allowed. As other models of decriminalization have emerged, and 2010 was marked by a wave of legalization. The first was Uruguay, which established a cannabis club system. Then Canada legalized the cultivation and sale of cannabis retail, defying international restrictions.

3 December 2020 - The UN deletes cannabis from the list of the most dangerous drugs

A definitive green light for the use of medical cannabis: the news that could finally mark a turning point regarding legalization is in recent days: the UN has in fact chosen to eliminate medical marijuana from the list of the most dangerous drugs, which includes drugs such as heroin and cocaine.

The Commission for Narcotic Drugs, based in Vienna, which includes 53 member states, has finally developed and approved a series of recommendations promoted by the World Health Organization such as eliminating cannabis from Table IV of the 1961 Single Convention, where hemp sativa appeared from 1961.

This was a long-awaited victory obtained by the UN and perhaps it could finally represent the first step to enhance and improve scientific research on cannabis and its therapeutic use now so widespread.

The legalization of cannabis in Europe

Legalization in Spain

Although Spanish law is quite tolerant and provides a considerable margin of freedom, possession of cannabis in Spain is not always legal. Drug dealing is a criminal offense and, in any case, prison sentences are also given if you choose to follow the path of illegality. The consumption of marijuana for personal use is often tolerated by the police within certain limits. Smoking marijuana is allowed but is considered something strictly private and personal that can only take place in one's home or in places specifically used: otherwise, consumption in a public place is considered a punishable offense at the discretion of the police with fines that can reach €300.

Discreet transport linked only to products packaged and certified by the manufacturer for quantities of less than or equal to 50 grams is also tolerated. However, Spanish cannabis law can vary depending on the location: just think of the freedom of Barcelona or Catalonia. Smoking in public is not permitted except for licensed clubs.

Legalization in France

In France the use of light cannabis is now considered illegal: however, the country has recently started the legalization process aimed solely at medical cannabis in a controlled manner and in anticipation of more radical measures. The imminent start of a marijuana legalization process is therefore desirable in order to provide users with legal access to a specific type of weed for purely medical use without social repercussions, planning such an "experiment" for the next two years.

Legalization in the Netherlands

Coffeeshops have been well known in the Netherlands for over 40 years, a reality made possible by the particular tolerance regime launched in the 70s by the Dutch government and confirmed by successive ones over the last fifty years. Although the production of cannabis and its marketing is formally illegal, the sale of small quantities within the premises is allowed only to adults. However, cultivation and distribution are still illegal and punishable as they are mainly controlled by the local underworld. Hiring in public is also a crime.

Legalization in Sweden

Although Sweden appears among the most liberal countries in Europe, the consumption of marijuana is currently not tolerated in any way. Particularly severe are the penalties therefore for the employers, even the possession of minimal quantities of weed risks heavy penalties and, in serious cases, imprisonment inside the country.

Legalization in Switzerland

In Switzerland, cannabis consumption is now considered illegal as is its sale and production, especially in the form of good weed or hashish. The consumption of hemp by adults is punished with a fine of 100 francs. Possession of quantities of less than 10 grams is not punishable while as regards minors the penalty provided may vary according to juvenile criminal law.

Legalization in Germany

Since March 2017, a law has been passed in Germany that offers the opportunity to prescribe cannabis to seriously ill patients, as a support to pain therapy. However, this law currently has a flaw due to the lack of parameters aimed at indicating and classifying the real severity of the disease. The consumption of light cannabis is usually legal but with obvious limitations related to the quantities in the possession of the user: depending on the region, it is possible to hold an amount ranging from 15 grams in Berlin to ⅗ grams in other regions.

Legalization in the UK

The United Kingdom is still a real laggard: to date, and only since last year, the use of cannabis in the therapeutic field has been authorized while keeping the consumption of weed for recreational purposes illegal. However, significant future changes are desirable in what appears to be the most tolerant country in terms of sanctions.

The legalization of cannabis in non-European countries

The legalization of cannabis in what are non-European countries seems to be a reason for much less heated discussions and debates than in Europe. A radically more open mindset allows jurisdictions a higher margin of tolerance, leading to consider weed, fortunately, no longer a taboo.

Legalization in Australia

In Australia, a recent provision established all the rules related to the consumption and possession of cannabis for recreational use, formalizing the effective legalization: adults have the right to own up to 50 grams of weed and can grow 2 plants each or 4 per family. Being a federal state, however, this law only involves the territory of the capital although since 2016 the consumption of marijuana for therapeutic purposes has also been legalized.

Legalization in California

California has also gradually adapted to the legalization process for cannabis: starting from January 1, 2019, the recreational use of marijuana became legal following a referendum held in November. Citizens over the age of 21 can freely own up to 28 grams of weed and grow up to six seedlings at home. However, hiring in public places is prohibited.

Legalization in the United States

On June 25, 2019, the Governor of Illinois approved the law by which the legalization of the use and sale of cannabis throughout the state took place in effect, starting from January 1, 2020. To date, this represents the 11th state in the US to have fully legalized marijuana, in the footsteps of Alaska, California, Colorado, Maine, Massachusetts, Michigan, Nevada, Oregon, Vermont and Washington. However, the number of states where it is considered legal to sell and buy marijuana increases if we also include the District of Columbia, where private sale is prohibited, and the territories of the Northern Mariana Islands and Guam. Quite curious if you think that prohibition was first seen in the United States!

THE MODERN MARIJUANA THERAPEUTIC

In the 19th century, European doctors such as William Brooke O'Shaughnessy and Jacques-Joseph Moreau introduced cannabis from a scientific angle to the Western world. They recorded the various therapeutic effects offered by cannabis. Curiously, the substance began to be used to treat various ailments, even after it was forced into hiding in the 20th century.

During that time, the newly founded nation of Israel began researching the molecules and chemical compounds found in the cannabis plant. A team of Israeli scientists, led by Dr. Raphael Mechoulam, discovered how to synthesize cannabinoids such as THC and CBD.

In addition, he studied endocannabinoids and cannabinoid receptors in the human body. These researchers helped reveal the potential of cannabis for treating various ailments and diseases. Today, medical marijuana is used in people with cancer and undergoing chemotherapy; it is used in anorexic subjects because it causes appetite, and in inappetent subjects debilitated by chronic diseases, such as AIDS and multiple sclerosis; because it causes muscle relaxation that fights the stiffness that these diseases cause. It is used against Parkinson's disease. It is also used in the treatment of epileptic subjects. It also plays a role in the treatment of glaucoma, since it lowers intraocular pressure.

CHAPTER 2: LEGAL CANNABIS AROUND THE WORLD: A PATCHY REALITY

Hemp continues to be the most persecuted plant in the world. This seems a strange thing, how can a plant be outlawed? Yet it is.

Cannabis suddenly became public enemy number one in 1937 when America banned the production, trade and use of hemp by enacting the Marijuana Act. The United States was not the first to embark on this reckless war: before them Egypt, Jamaica and South Africa had thought about it, while in Italy it was Mussolini who banned the cultivation and use of cannabis forever. Despite this, the American stance is remembered as the highlight of this absurd prohibition, as the law was accompanied by a shameful press campaign, which forever associated the use of this plant with deviant behavior. Also tinged with a subtle as well as ferocious racism, American propaganda planted the seeds of what, in the following years, became the social and political orientation towards cannabis and those who use it.

The ban quickly spread like wildfire, affecting not only Western countries, but also the states in which marijuana was a full part of the uses and traditions of the peoples who, among other things, had always cultivated it.

Since then, hemp has been the first outlawed plant in history and still is today in most of the world.

Yet, the first timid signs of change appear on the horizon and the debate on the effectiveness, but above all on the meaning, of this new prohibitionism is increasingly lively and widespread.

To date, between quick pushes forward, timid openings and rigid conservatism, the laws on the possession and use of marijuana are decidedly diverse and range from total legalization to the very severe penalties still in force in some countries of Southeast Asia.

Let's see what the situation is in the world.

Legalized cannabis: where to smoke it without problems

To date, the only countries that have fully legalized cannabis are Uruguay and Canada.

The South American country will be remembered in the history books as the first state to have completely legalized the recreational use of marijuana: in 2013, raising a media fuss and a bitter global debate, President Jose Mujica signs a law which, thanks to subsequent changes, leads the country to be the first nation in the world where it is possible to produce, buy and consume hemp freely. But don't rush to buy a plane ticket to Montevideo: the use of cannabis for recreational uses is allowed only to Uruguayan citizens and residents, who must be registered in the national register of consumers.

In Canada, the legalization of hemp came in 2018 thanks to the Cannabis Act, which finally allows recreational use to all citizens of age. In some provinces it is only possible to buy marijuana from state-run businesses, while in others it is also allowed to purchase from individuals. Smoking marijuana is only allowed in private homes, although outdoor use and public parks are tolerated in some provinces. On the contrary, Canadian law harshly pursues those who drive while intoxicated: if you are stopped by the police, you may be subjected to tests to verify that the THC nanograms contained in your blood do not exceed the 5 established by law. Indoor cultivation is almost always allowed, as long as there are no more than 4 plants and strict protocols are followed to prevent children from coming into contact with cannabis.

The panorama of states that are slowly moving towards more permissive legislation, but have not yet made the big leap towards full legalization, is much wider. Here the situation is really confused and each country has adopted its own laws, with more or less paradoxical aspects.

The country that is most open to marijuana smokers, but also the one with the most schizophrenic legislation, is Holland. Contrary to what many of you think, cannabis is illegal in the Netherlands, although its use is tolerated nationwide. Strange, right? But if this sounds bizarre to you, wait until you hear what the real " backdoor problem " is, as the Dutch call it: as everyone knows, Holland is home to coffeeshops, but these businesses have to get their supplies from the black market. In practice, what they buy illegally suddenly becomes legally marketable from the moment it arrives at their facility. Insane? Yes, and this is the reason why, after a short period of tightening of the laws, which led to the closure of many coffeeshops, the situation is back as before and it seems quite obvious that, sooner or later, the government will legalize what has been done for a long time.

In the rest of Europe, the situation remains very varied. Although many states have opened up to the consumption of light hemp and cannabis for therapeutic purposes, recreational use remains strongly repressed. In some countries, such as Spain, the Czech Republic and Switzerland, the process towards legalization is further ahead than in others and, although not legalized, the possession of hemp is tolerated and decriminalized, as long as the quantity is within the limits set by law.

In the rest of Europe, if you want to buy cannabis, you do it at your own risk: the possession of hemp, if it falls within the so-called moderate quantity, is often tolerated by the police, but it is always better not to rely on it. In practice, holding, selling and growing marijuana remains a crime and penalties vary enormously from one country to another.

Where hemp is illegal and the penalties very severe

In the rest of the world, hemp remains totally illegal and penalties for offenders can reach up to life imprisonment, in cases of buying and selling large quantities. The paradoxical aspect of this type of legislation lies in the fact that it is adopted by countries which were traditionally producers and consumers of this plant. The quality of Indian and Nepalese hemp is famous all over the world, yet in these states the law is clear: production, possession and trade are totally prohibited. Just as the penalties are very severe in Malaysia,

Indonesia and all of South Asia, countries where the possession of a few grams of marijuana can lead to very long detention, not to mention international drug trafficking, for which the penalties go up to life imprisonment.

In Africa, hemp is illegal everywhere and if it is true that in many countries it is very easy to find it, be careful what you do: the police are usually complacent with the locals, but it is very likely that they are not with you. The only exception in the continent is South Africa, which in recent years has been trying the difficult road towards legalization, starting to decriminalize the possession of small quantities and the cultivation of cannabis inside homes.

The war that America began almost a century ago is not over yet and, although encouraging signs can be seen here and there, the road to the complete rehabilitation of hemp is still very long and full of obstacles. But, as often happens, the positions of governments are always much more backward than those of the voters: the popular consensus towards a decisive legalization of hemp is increasingly broad and it is not excluded that, in the coming years, many countries will find themselves having to do deals with the anti-prohibitionist pressures of millions of citizens, finally clearing the recreational use of a plant that has not received the treatment it deserved.

CHAPTER 3: WHERE IT IS GROWN

The United Nations Office on Drugs and Crime (UNODC) recently released its 2017 World Drug Report - the 20th annual survey on manufacturing, trafficking and eradication and enforcement efforts around the world.

In recent years, the report has sought to quantify the amount of cannabis grown in each producing country - over the past decade consistently placing Morocco first, generally followed by Mexico and Paraguay.

This general trend continues - with some new variations.

The report seeks only to quantify the cultivated area for the best producers.

Morocco is again at the head of the row, with 47,000 hectares dedicated to cannabis cultivation. It is followed by Mexico with 15,000 hectares.

But now the industry has arrived in Nigeria which settles in third place at just over 4,500 hectares. Followed closely by Lebanon with 3,500. Paraguay is just behind with 2,780.

There is some lag time in UNDOC reports, as they are based on the most recent figures available: the 2017 report is based on data collected between 2010 and 2015.

The estimates are based on "direct indicators (cultivation or eradication of cannabis plants) or indirect (seizures of cannabis plants, production of domestic cannabis as a source of seizures, etc.) ..."

The report acknowledged: "The extent is challenging because some countries report eradication in terms of hectares, while others report in terms of the number of uprooted cannabis plants, the weight of seized cannabis plants or the number of sites of cannabis cultivation that have been eradicated. This makes comparisons of eradication difficult".

If you look at the uprooted area, first is Mexico, followed by Morocco and Nigeria, based on the 2010-2015 figures.

The largest number of cannabis growing sites were found in the United States, followed by Ukraine, the Netherlands and Russia.

The largest number of eradicated cannabis plants were reported from Nigeria, followed by the United States, the Philippines and Paraguay.

The largest quantities of cannabis plants seized were reported from Bolivia and Peru, followed by Jamaica.

In terms of tons of "cannabis weed" seized, the United States is in the lead, followed by Mexico, Paraguay, Colombia and Nigeria. For tons of "cannabis resin", Spain is the global leader (contraband from North Africa), followed by Pakistan, Morocco, Afghanistan and Algeria.

Unsurprisingly, more hash is "taken" in the Old World while more herbaceous cannabis is "taken" in the New World. In 2015, nearly two-thirds (64 percent) of the total amount of cannabis flowers seized around the world were seized in the Americas, according to the report.

Cannabis

Consumer market in Europe

It is estimated that more than 80 million adults have used cannabis at least once; of these over 22 million have done so in the last year. Based on these data, cannabis is by far the most widely consumed illicit drug in the EU. On reflection, the estimated market value of cannabis is very high, coming in at over €9 billion. About 1% of European adults are believed to consume cannabis daily, or almost. It is this group of individuals that raises the greatest concern in relation to the potential health and social problems associated with such consumption. National trends in cannabis use highlighted by recent surveys differ from each other, showing both increases and decreases. However, cannabis is currently the most frequently reported drug as the primary reason for first access to drug addiction therapies and the second most frequently cited substance among all patients on treatment. Cannabis is commonly available in Europe in two distinct forms: the leaves and the resin. Either way, it is usually smoked alongside tobacco, creating additional potential health impacts. The reported retail prices for cannabis resin and leaves are currently very similar, typically ranging between 7 and 12 EURO per gram. However, prices vary by country, as does the perceived quality of the product. Although prices have only risen slightly over the past decade, the average potency in terms of tetrahydrocannabinol (THC) has almost doubled over the same period.

Products and market innovation. Cannabis production in the EU over the past decade has led to a change in the market: in many countries, home-made leaf products have become more relevant at the expense of imported resin. That said, imported resin remains important and continues to enter the EU. Cannabis leaves enter from several other potential source countries. Internal production takes place in various forms, ranging from small-scale cultivation for personal use to large plantations. Although some large-scale crops are located outdoors, intensive cultivation sites are often located indoors or underground and can pose a significant fire hazard. The use of intensive and sophisticated in-house production techniques, together with the availability of high-potency strains of the cannabis plant, is probably one of the factors that have led to the increase in potency of both resins and leaf products observed in recent years. It seems that many cannabis users equate potency with quality, thus resulting in a particular demand and appreciation for high potency products. As there is sufficient competition in the market, this phenomenon acts as an incentive for Moroccan resin producers, who have introduced new hybrid varieties of the plant with high potency and high yield.

Although data on other forms of cannabis available on the European market are scarce, evidence from other contexts, in particular that of the United States, suggest that there is ample room for innovation in the future, especially with regard to edible products, and oils or cannabis intended for use in vaporizers. In historical terms, small quantities of cannabis oil have been sporadically available on the EU market; however, recent reports of domestic production using butane gas from the United States are worrying from both public health and public safety standpoints. More generally, the existence of a large legitimate commercial cannabis market in the United States is likely to lead to more product innovation, with a possible ripple effect in the EU. However, EU internal production is already supported from physical sales points and online, that sell products such as audio-visual equipment and lighting, and kits for the production of resin. Some very high potency resins of domestic production have recently been detected and the future commercial production of very potent cannabis resins in the EU is now a real possibility. A link between some cannabis grow shops and criminal groups involved in the trafficking and sale of cannabis has led to recent businesses in the Czech Republic and the Netherlands to target this type of business. Nonetheless, such measures may result in a shift of business to neighboring countries or the online market.

Between cannabis and organized crime

The somewhat benign public image of the cannabis market derived from the activities of hippy entrepreneurs in the 1960s stands in stark contrast to modern reality.

Crime or organized groups currently play an important role in a large sector that generates financial flows associated with violence and other forms of crime.

Furthermore, the vast reach of the cannabis market makes it important for criminal activities at all levels. For example, street gangs are often involved in retail and sometimes manufacturing, which has led to gang conflicts in some European Member States. The negative impacts of the large illicit cannabis market on local communities and law enforcement resources, as well as the resulting costs, are often overlooked. Moroccan organized crime groups, which exploit the links with Moroccan communities in Europe and collaborate with European groups, have an established role in the import of large quantities of cannabis resin. Spain, the Netherlands and, to a lesser extent, Belgium are the main import and distribution points for the entire EU market. These activities continue to lead to gang violence in some countries.

However, it was probably the growth in domestic cannabis production that caused most of the clashes between the groups. Large indoor production sites are linked to violent crime between groups, as well as the theft of electricity, and are also associated with trafficking in human beings. Migrants and victims of human trafficking, as well as other vulnerable people, have been employed, sometimes with coercive measures, to work at production sites. Although many groups are involved, the Dutch and Vietnamese organized crime groups in particular have built up an international reputation as a major player in this sector.

Some of these groups have set up their own cannabis production sites outside their home country, while others provide know-how and equipment to groups in other countries, encouraging the spread of domestic cannabis production to new locations.

In terms of market developments, Spain, traditionally the main entry point for resin produced in Morocco, has recently reported an increase in seizures of cannabis leaves, suggesting an increase in local production. Seizures of cannabis leaves are also on the rise in Italy and in Greece. In addition, Turkey reported in 2013 that it seized 180 tons of cannabis leaves, more than all EU countries combined. However, the implications of such seizures for the EU market are unclear. A recent development has also been the limited appearance, in some parts of the EU, of Afghan resin, which Albanian groups are associated with. Albania is also an important country of origin for cannabis leaves arriving in the EU. Some recent interceptions of large batches of cannabis resin moving east along the North African coast are also worrying, as they may signal the emergence of new trafficking routes through southern European countries and the Western Balkans, with potential links to trafficking in human beings, or to unstable regions of the eastern Mediterranean.

188 million people used cannabis in 2017, with production coming from 159 different countries and, mainly, from the Maghreb, Mashrek and the southern Balkans. A number that makes you think this is the most widely used substance in the world, with a growth trend in North America (up 60% from 2007 to 2017) and in Asia. The Americas are also where the substance is seized the most. South America

represented 38% of the world total in 2017, while North America 21%, a figure in sharp decline compared to 2016 mainly due to the effect of legalization for non-medical use of the substance in some states.

The trend also suggests an increase in both indoor and outdoor growing, with indoor growing closely associated with a general increase in THC levels compared to two decades ago.

Furthermore, in the last decade, cannabis products have increased, which tend to be rich in THC (one of the best-known active ingredients in cannabis) and low in CBD. In Europe alone, the average THC content of cannabis resin has doubled from around 8 percent in 2006 to 17 percent in 2016, and the THC content of cannabis herbs has increased from 5 to 10 percent over the same period. According to the World Drug Report 2019, "it is believed that when CBD and THC are administered in balanced proportions, CBD may be able to reduce some of the effects of THC, such as anxiety and paranoia."

The most recent overview of cannabis use in every single country and globally indicates that the strategy of repression and prohibition has failed to prevent the use of THC and other psychoactive substances by the population.

CONSUMPTION OF CANNABIS IS A GLOBAL NEED

Towards the end of each year, local and international agencies release data on drug use, crimes occurring, unemployment rate, fake inflation data, and everything needed to be good informed citizens. The use of all types of psychotropic drugs, legal and illegal, has been steadily increasing for decades in almost all nations. The use of cannabis is rampant as a medicine, spiritual aid, and a substitute for other more dangerous substances. Fun fact: there is no direct relationship between local laws and cannabis use. People consume cannabis all over the world, despite the laws.

The authoritative United Nation Office on Drugs and Crime has just published some figures on cannabis use around the world. Some caution should be exercised in reading these numbers, because they have been obtained with different research methods and come from different agencies. That is why we prefer to aggregate this information to provide an overall picture rather than drawing up a Top 10 ranking. The winner is Iceland, however. Not those stoners you thought.

UNODC data shows that Iceland is one of the countries with the largest number of cannabis users. The reason is unclear, or it could be that beer was made legal 25 years ago and alcoholic beverages are very expensive. The figures indicate that 18.3% of the Icelandic population aged 15 to 64 use cannabis. Not bad as a result, about one in five adult smokers. Even a small African nation shows a high percentage, with 21.5% smokers, or 5.8 million people. Ghana is the sixth largest cannabis user in the world, and ranks second in percentage of the number of citizens. Cannabis is almost as illegal in Ghana as it is in France, where governments continue to increase penalties for possessing cannabis. Despite this, more than 11% of the French consume cannabis, which is equivalent to 6 million smokers. They are among the largest consumers of weed in Europe, and rank 7th in the world. Voila.

Spain, on the other hand, is one of the leading exponents of drug reform, following a model of decriminalization rather than punishment and incarceration. In Spain it is not legal to grow cannabis for personal use, and even cannabis club experiments live in a gray area of legality. Despite the official status of legality, the use of cannabis for personal and social purposes is tolerated, and sometimes the authorities turn a blind eye to patients who grow their own marijuana for medical use.

Official data indicate that 10.6% of Spaniards consume cannabis. Nobody believes it, and some place the figure over 25%, even higher than in Ghana. Spain continues to follow its normalization path: Another major city is regulating cannabis, and the whole nation will prepare a special law to allow cannabis clubs to operate legally.

The policies can lead to different outcomes, such as the Netherlands is around twentieth in the world rankings. In the US, medical cannabis is legal in over 20 states, for a wide range of conditions. Recreational use is legal in four states, and the number will increase over the next few months or years. The percentage of users could be 14% or 16%, lower than in Zambia, which reaches 17.7%. The Americans therefore showed their love for cannabis by smoking it and spreading its derivatives. Translated into numbers, this passion involves around 44 million people. In absolute numbers, this is obviously the nation with the highest number of stoners.

Among the group of nations that report cannabis use by around 15% of the population, we find Nigeria with 14.3% of users. The same percentage of Italy, which is the nation with the highest cannabis consumption in Europe. The possession of small quantities of cannabis is decriminalized, but the trade is fully punished, with the result that 14.6% of Italians smoke cannabis, or 8.9 million people. Italy ranks fourth in the world in terms of number of consumers. New Zealand has roughly the same percentage of smokers as Italy, while Canada only reaches 12%. Here the government issues licenses for medical and industrial use, and the recreational use of cannabis is highly tolerated. Australia has 10.2% smoking users, more than Jamaica, which, believe it or not, only has 7.2% smokers.

Some producers don't consume what they produce, others do. It seems that Pakistan has only 3.9% of consumers, not many, but equivalent to 7.6 million people, ranking 5th in the world. Furthermore, only 6.2% of 88 million Egyptians smoke cannabis, or 5.4 million people, at the 8th position in the world rankings. Cannabis is illegal in these countries, as well as in India, where it is widely consumed in various regions. Only 3.2% of Indians smoke cannabis, but the figures are based on a population of over 1.2 billion, so that is 38.5 million people. Albania doesn't even make it into the top 30 cannabis smoking nations, despite being the scene of a bloody war over cannabis.

We therefore draw up a possible list of the 30 main cannabis smoking nations, according to official UNODC data in percentages, referring to the total adult population.

Looking at the figures, we can easily deduce that 10% of the world's population uses cannabis, or would be willing to consume it, if weed were more available. The number of these patients is constantly increasing, and could mean 500 million individuals consuming 1 gram of cannabis per day at an average price of 10 Euros per gram. This would mean 50 billion euros burned per day, over 18 trillion euros per year. This amount is equivalent to the Gross Domestic Product of the entire European Union. Here's what these figures will ultimately mean if the cultivation of cannabis for personal or aggregative use is not fully legalized.

CHAPTER 4 LEGAL MARIJUANA

WHAT *distinguishes legal marijuana from non-legal marijuana?*

In summary, the main difference is simply in the concentration of a substance (THC), which is naturally present in the plant and which must be contained on particularly low thresholds.

In fact, we recall that in legal cannabis this concentration must be equal to or less than 0.6% in Italy, and that on the other hand all products that exceed this threshold are considered illegal, as well as capable of impacting human health with their effects on the body.

The distinction criteria mentioned above should represent a good alarm bell for those who want to buy safe products, as well as a deep line of demarcation between legal products and those that would expose users to prejudicial consequences, from a criminal point of view. In addition, the illegal derivatives often do not carry any information on the packaging, while the safe and legal products have all the real and transparent information on how to use the product, the amount of THC and the origin of the plant (as well as the identification of the manufacturing company).

It does not escape us, in fact, that in the legal marijuana sector it is traceability that is the real strength. In the purchasing process, therefore, maximum attention must be paid to the shop you're in, which is its operational and legal headquarters and, above all, to what information on the treatments and processing processes that the material has received, before hitting the shelves or an e-commerce site.

We also remember some that distribute legal cannabis - and that can sell some of the most purchased types of light cannabis - can also be franchises, and that it is always advisable - even in this case - to find out who the supplier of the products is. This formula allows you to understand who are the operators involved and responsible for each phase of the supply chain that goes from the producer to the purchase order in total transparency.

Well, having introduced the above, in this guide, you will find out everything you need to know about legal cannabis: the legislation, what a shop must do to be legal, what products to choose and how to recognize them, and of course what is the difference between the products for therapeutic use and those for recreational use and how the Italian law works to mark this difference.

LEGAL MARIJUANA: THE LEGISLATION

Legal Cannabis: Difference Between Therapeutic Use and Recreational Use

It is necessary to mention the difference between therapeutic and recreational use of cannabis, which closely follows the distinction between legal and illegal cannabis.

Medical cannabis is in fact the one necessary as an element and raw material useful for creating drugs. Therefore, medical supervision is constant throughout the production process and the presence of this substance is clearly indicated on the packaging and on the product leaflet. In addition, these products are strictly controlled by AIFA, the Medicines Agency and, for these reasons, they are not sold freely on the market, but only upon presentation of a prescription from a specialist. Naturally, it will be necessary to go to facilities managed by the local ASL to proceed with the withdrawal.

Recreational cannabis, on the other hand, is dangerous to health if it exceeds the legal limits. With the term recreational, in fact, we go to classify those products that are used "to have fun", and therefore present themselves as substances that offer the "easy high".

All those products that are ultimately not for medical use, and for which therefore no prescription is required, are classified as legal cannabis. However, they are not for recreational use as they do not cause any effect, and are therefore to be considered fully safe for health. Among the products that fall under legal cannabis in Italy there are perfumers for rooms or for the person, oils, inflorescences and clothing. Their main task is to allow users to benefit from all the relaxing properties of hemp without fear of the negative effects!

CHAPTER 5: COFFEE SHOP, SMART SHOP, DISPENSARIES

Coffeeshop, headshop, smartshop and dispensaries ... All terms that you may have already read and that may have confused you a bit. We will quickly analyze the differences between these types of retailers and what you can expect from each of them.

In some countries, people are still forced to buy weed on the street or through shady back channels, provided you have the courage and / or the desire to break the law. This situation is downright unpleasant for cannabis enthusiasts who live in, or visit, these areas. Thankfully, a growing number of countries around the world are adopting a more tolerant approach to using and buying and selling cannabis.

The type of "cannabis supplier" you will need to interact with depends mainly on the country you are in. Flowers, for therapeutic or recreational use, and in some places even concentrates, are sold in various shops, each following their own rules of engagement.

COFFEESHOPS: DUTCH SHOPS THAT SELL CANNABIS

The coffeeshops are an invention of the Netherlands and a major tourist attraction of the Netherlands. In the 1970s, the Dutch government decided to change its stance on drugs, largely decriminalizing the use of cannabis. This initiative gave birth to the Dutch coffeeshop scene, now internationally recognized.

The atmosphere at the coffee shops varies from place to place, as do the prices and quality of the weed sold. Most of Amsterdam's coffeeshops are located in the red-light district and cater mainly to tourists. However, there are other less touristy coffeeshops hidden throughout the city.

Almost all coffeeshops offer a large selection of cannabis inflorescences, extracts and even edibles. These stores are licensed by the government and must be subject to a number of restrictions. For example, under Dutch law governing coffeeshops, a store can only sell a maximum of 5g of cannabis twice a day to the same person. They also cannot sell cigarettes or alcohol.

HEADSHOP AND SMARTSHOP: FROM PHYSICAL STORES TO ELECTRONIC COMMERCE

The headshop can still be found in many countries. They usually sell bongs, pipes, rolling papers, grinders, and other cannabis-related accessories and tools. In the United States, during the hippie movement of the 1960s, headshops began to appear across the country and many of them had ties to socio-political movements against drug prohibition, the Vietnam War and more.

Smartshops, however, are more recent and usually are dedicated to the sale of psychoactive substances and related products. They are very popular in the Netherlands, where they can legally sell psychoactive truffles and cacti. However, they are also found in Sweden, the United Kingdom, the Republic of Ireland and Portugal. The latter maintains a very liberal stance on drugs.

Today, physical head / smartshop stores have largely been converted into online businesses.

DISPENSARY: THE AMERICAN METHOD

Dispensaries are a commercial reality that exists only in the United States, although in Canada some retailers have labeled themselves as dispensaries. In the United States, dispensaries are regulated by the local government and, according to local laws, can sell certain quantities of cannabis products.

Dispensaries can only sell cannabis to adult customers (in states with laws on recreational use intended for an adult audience) or for therapeutic purposes. In the latter case, cannabis can only be sold to those with a medical prescription or registered as a patient on medical marijuana treatment.

US dispensaries offer a variety of cannabis products, including extracts, tinctures, vape cartridges, food items and, of course, a large selection of dried buds. In some states, dispensaries even sell clones and plants. The amount of marijuana that a dispensary can legally sell in a single transaction varies from state to state.

COLLECTIVES: NON-PROFIT ORGANIZATIONS

Cannabis collectives differ from dispensaries in that they are usually non-profit organizations. Like existing collectives in other sectors, these organizations are made up of a group of people who work for a common goal, which is to provide cannabis to those in need for therapeutic reasons or to adult buyers. Collectives of this type usually offer the same products as dispensaries. However, in some cases, they may only sell cannabis to their members or patients registered within the collective, it all depends on the local laws in which the organization is operating.

CANNABIS CLUB: THE SOLUTION FOR ADULTS ONLY IN SPAIN AND URUGUAY

Cannabis clubs are very popular in Uruguay and Spain. These clubs are usually registered non-profit organizations to produce cannabis for their members.

In Spain, new members can only join a club on the recommendation of another member. In general, members can purchase a maximum daily amount of around 3g of cannabis, in order to prevent resale.

In Uruguay, registered clubs can produce a certain amount of cannabis per month for each member, who usually has to pay a monthly membership fee. These clubs are also registered as private non-profit organizations.

CHAPTER 6: HOW TO GET INTO THE LEGAL
MARIJUANA BUSINESS

Entering the marijuana and legal hemp business, therefore light, represents an interesting opportunity, no doubt to be taken into consideration. Light marijuana is a natural product, which is obtained from the female flowers of hemp plants that have a very low level of THC.

Hemp with low or even insignificant THC levels cannot be equated with drugs, due to the fact that it does not alter the psyche. After years of research and attempts, the experts in the field have in fact succeeded in their intent to originate varieties of plants not able to be called drugs.

These plants are cannabis varieties that have a THC value that should not exceed 0.2%, although exceeding this limit by up to 0.6% is tolerated by law.

Marijuana obtained from light hemp is a highly sought-after product, especially due to the fact that it contains CBD (cannabidiol), a substance that gives a feeling of relaxation, and which according to various studies is also able to offer many others benefits.

But how to become a light cannabis reseller? There are various avenues to choose from, between physical and online stores, and there are also various types of opportunities to buy wholesale hemp and then resell it.

HOW TO BECOME A LIGHT CANNABIS DEALER

No special certifications or specific permits are required to become a light cannabis reseller. In fact, it is possible to do it in the same way as you can open a bar, a grocery store, a mobile phone shop, a tobacconist, etc.

However, it is advisable to have specific skills in the sector, such as an in-depth knowledge of the cannabis products sold, and their target market. And it is also crucial to consider whether to sell in physical stores and / or through online stores.

Furthermore, there are also other issues to consider to set up this business:

Cannabis and light marijuana to be marketed must be accompanied by a special certificate of origin, which certifies the place of origin and quality of the seeds used for cultivation. In particular, the plant varieties judged light are those present in the Common Catalog of the European Union: there are 67 different species, all with a very low THC content.

Light cannabis and light marijuana must also have a laboratory certificate, certifying the values of all the main substances they contain. This document must always be attached to the sale, both wholesale and retail.

The packs of light marijuana must also have information relating to the batch of origin.

Such packages must also be sealed and hermetically sealed, whether they are sold individually at retail or in the case of wholesale supplies.

OPEN A LEGAL MARIJUANA STORE

As for the sale of cannabis and light marijuana in physical stores, there are some commercial activities that can do so. If you already have an established business, such as a grow shop, for the sale of products obtained from light hemp you can contact a supplier.

If, on the other hand, you decide to start from scratch, to dedicate yourself to the sale of products obtained with light hemp, in addition to contacting a supplier it is also necessary to take care of the appropriate opening of a physical store.

For example, you can open a hemp shop: it is a form of grow shop dedicated more specifically to the sale of hemp-based products.

To proceed in opening a hemp shop, there are some steps to follow, including:

Open a VAT number and a current account.

Rent or buy a place to do business.

Make the start of business communication (SCIA) to the trade office of the Municipality, which in the case of hemp shops concerns the sale of flowers and products derived from cannabis.

Respect the safety, urban planning and hygiene regulations.

Choose the supplier (or wholesaler) regardless of nationality. However, we must also keep in mind that the further away from the shop, the longer it will take for the goods to arrive.

For completeness of information, below we explain in more detail what a wholesaler does: he sells products in large quantities at lower prices than those found in stores, to allow retailing to those who have a store, physical and / or online.

Retailing, on the other hand, is the activity of the retailer, who must sell the goods purchased by the wholesaler to the final consumer.

Another, more convenient, possibility to open a physical shop than hemp shop is to contact a franchising company: taking advantage of this opportunity, you rely on a company that generally carries out most of the bureaucratic activities for the opening, while the shopkeeper will mainly have to deal with finding a place, managing it, and dedicating himself to the sale of the products that are supplied from time to time.

Buy hemp wholesale and resell it online

In addition to the possibility of opening a physical store, there is also one that allows you to sell cannabis light products through an online store.

Also, with regard to virtual shops, for the sale of the goods it is necessary to contact a wholesaler, that is a supplier who sells products to the retailer.

After purchasing light hemp products to resell them on the net, it is necessary to propose the goods to be sold to the public through a special website.

In addition, taking advantage of the potential offered by the network, it is possible to use various online tools to increase your clientele, with various types of online marketing initiatives that help to obtain greater visibility for your business.

HOW TO BUY WHOLESALE HEMP

Those who choose to become a light cannabis reseller, whether in a physical store, an online store, or both, have a valid ally on the internet. In fact, on the web it is possible to find several sites that offer wholesale sales.

These are usually reliable wholesalers, offering products from legal cannabis grown under controlled conditions or outdoors, in climatic areas suitable for this type of crop.

By doing a search on Google, typing for example "light hemp wholesalers", as results you will get several sites that you can rely on, after registration. By accessing these sites, it is possible to obtain contact details (telephone, e-mail, etc.) with which you can get in touch for precise information on how to establish a collaborative relationship.

Furthermore, starting from each of these sites it is possible to consult the relative pages to see what type of products they offer, how much they sell them, and where their company headquarters and the goods offered are located.

However, choosing the supplier is only one of the steps to be taken in order to resell legal cannabis products online. Another important step is related to the opening of the online store, as better explained in the next paragraph.

HOW TO OPEN A LEGAL CANNABIS ONLINE SHOP

There are two possibilities to open a legal cannabis online store: do it as a franchise or on your own.

In case you already have a business in a physical store, the choice to make may also depend on the way in which you are already operating. While, in the event that you do not have an online store at the same time, perhaps the ideal solution is to rely on a franchising service, also because in the latter case it is not even necessary to establish agreements with a wholesaler. In addition, online wholesalers are sometimes also franchise sellers.

It is good to highlight the main advantages of opening an online store compared to a physical store:

Fewer expenses: there is no need to buy or rent a room, furnish it, and hire staff to manage it. In this sense, the costs are significantly lowered.

Ability to reach a wider audience than those who live nearby. Furthermore, it is also possible to serve a clientele who would never go to a physical store dedicated to the sale of light cannabis.

Opportunity to sell anytime, any day of the year.

Possibility to ask for an e-mail to those who make purchases on the site, so as to send discounts and promotions directly to their e-mail inbox, in order to facilitate the possibility that they return to buy in the online shop.

Here are the advantages of opening an online store in franchising instead of on your own:

The possibility of always receiving the goods from the best producers, and therefore of offering customers a wide choice of very interesting and certainly legal products.

The opportunity to have at your disposal an already known brand, namely the franchising one. All this will have significant implications, since an already known brand is perceived by end consumers as a sign of reliability, right from the first day of opening the online store.

Less stressful management of the warehouse: procurement of goods and management of unsold items can be carried out in a much simpler way, and with less expense.

The possibility of receiving assistance and help in case of need, from competent personnel.

How to increase the visibility and profits of the legal marijuana online store

When opening any website that sells products, of whatever type they are, it is also very important to understand how to encourage the purchase, and how to obtain adequate visibility that allows you to reach a large number of people interested in the goods.

For the purposes described above, the site used should have the following characteristics:

A simple navigation interface: if the site is easy to use, customers tend to buy with pleasure, and the likelihood that they will return to make other purchases in the future increases.

A search box, and a subdivision of products by categories: in this way, anyone who accesses can view the products available in a faster way.

Multiple payment systems: credit cards, PayPal, etc. so that all users can pay in the way that is possible or more convenient for them.

Detailed information on the light cannabis products sold, including the levels of THC and CBD they contain: transparency with respect to what is sold is highly appreciated by customers, who when they see a wide availability of information on what is offered, they feel in safer hands.

Optimization of the site for search through Google and other search engines: as regards this operation, if you are not an expert on the subject, it is better to rely on SEO specialists. Optimizing your site is essential nowadays if the goal is to sell more. In fact, people usually turn to search engines when they search for something on the web, and they generally choose the first results they see appear.

A section in which to offer more information about your account, and from which city the goods being sold come from.

A possible section for a blog, that is, a space for informative articles relating to your business, any discounts and promotions, news on the subject of cannabis, and useful advice for consumers relating to the purchase and use of legal cannabis.

Furthermore, to obtain greater visibility it is also highly recommended to open social channels.

On Instagram it is possible, for example, to periodically publish photos of the products sold, and at the same time illustrate any discounts and promotions in progress.

On Facebook, in addition to what is also possible with Instagram, you can also publish any content from your blog of the online site, the one with which the sale of light marijuana products is also carried out.

Again, with regard to social media, it is very important to publish content with a certain frequency, also because in this way people are able to remember if necessary, the existence of the online store to promote.

Another system to obtain visibility is to make a request to appear on the advertising banners of the various sites with advertising.

Yet another is to be sponsored by influencers (charismatic and / or competent people in a certain topic, who are followed on social networks), or by certain blogs or other sites that practice affiliate marketing, an activity that consists of creating content in which certain products to be purchased are strategically proposed.

CHAPTER 7: WHAT IT TAKES TO OPEN A SHOP

What Does It Take to Get a License to Grow or Sell Cannabis?

Are you thinking of entering the cannabis industry? If you want to become a commercial grower or if you like the idea of opening a dispensary, know that you will have to bear a mountain of costs and legal requirements. Find out what to expect if you want to get a license to sell cannabis in America, Canada and Europe.

The cannabis industry is booming. New cannabis companies and outlets are opening at an impressive pace in many places. It might seem like an easy industry to break into, but the reality is very different. In short: it takes a long time to get a license to sell cannabis, and we're not just referring to very high taxes. Below we discuss the main factors to consider when considering applying for a commercial license for cannabis in the United States, Canada, and Europe.

FACTORS TO TAKE INTO CONSIDERATION IF YOU WANT TO JOIN CANNABUSINESS AND KNOW LOCAL LAWS AND REGULATIONS

It doesn't matter if you want to get a license to farm or to open a dispensary, the starting point is to consider the legal aspects. Despite the "youth" of the legal cannabis industry, the barrier to entry is actually very high and the requirements stringent. That is why it is imperative that you know all local laws and regulations. Markets for legal cannabis vary widely and can either favor or prevent the success of those who accept this challenge.

Criminal background checks are often required, not just for a dispensary owner, for example, but also for all employees and investors. In some places, such as Canada, growing commercial medical cannabis requires all managers to have a valid permit. So, if you have a criminal background, your dreams of hitting the market big as a licensed medical grower may vanish before you even begin.

Then there are the gray areas, which are complex to navigate. "Tolerated" or "decriminalized" does not mean that marijuana is legal. And if it's not legal, or local laws aren't clear and your city council hasn't passed anything explicitly authorizing the cultivation of recreational cannabis, that means a dispensary could be shut down by the government at any time. And you usually don't want to risk an investment in something that is still illegal in the eyes of the state.

You should not only be aware of current laws, but future ones as well. This young industry has a lot of legislative proposals to consider, so there are likely to be changes in the regulations. Staying ahead in this game by trying to understand future developments will make the process smoother.

Likewise, you need to be aware that some places, like the United States for example, have cannabis laws that put individual states in conflict with federal power. At the federal level, cannabis is still illegal and is classified as a Schedule 1 drug in the United States, while legal cannabis flourishes in individual states.

So, first of all make sure you prioritize research. Even better, consult an experienced attorney in the field and follow their advice.

PREPARE A BUSINESS PLAN

On paper, there is nothing more attractive than the prospect of turning a hobby into a business. But with the saturation of numerous niches in the cannabis market, such as the CBD sector, many people who enter the field quickly find themselves in difficulty, not only due to the high requirements and legal uncertainties, but also due to a lack of skills. and professional experience.

If you want to be successful you have to be professional. A solid business plan is a great first step in this direction. A well-made plan will help you in several ways. First, show that you are serious about your business and that you understand the intricacies of what you are about to do. It also works as a personal roadmap for keeping things organized and under control, especially in the early stages. Finally, a business plan is key when trying to get investor finance. These people want to understand if they will ultimately make a return on their investment.

YOU NEED CAPITAL TO START

As a matter of fact, you need capital to start a business. Your business plan should indicate how you will access this capital and what it will be used for. This can be a major challenge as not only is funding of between $ 200,000 and $ 250,000 as a minimum, but also because a bank is unlikely to guarantee a loan. You can thank the legal gray areas for that. Therefore, it is necessary to obtain financing through other methods, for example from investors or private capital.

Your business plan should also list the future running costs for your business. This will include annual license fees, rental costs, employee salaries, transportation costs and any other expenses.

FIND A SUITABLE OFFICE

There are not only special requirements for obtaining a license, but those who start a company in the cannabis sector must also follow some operational rules. To work as a dispensary in California you can't just rent a space wherever you like. There are strict rules on how far cannabis outlets must be from schools, churches and residential areas.

Similarly, it is necessary to maintain a high level of security for any type of premises where cannabis is stored. For example, there are some regulations that dictate that walls must be of a certain thickness, along with other security specifications that add to the cost and energy needed to support the business. To be accepted, your commercial grow license application in Canada must include a detailed description of the site, its floor plans, and the safety measures applied.

FEES AND LICENSE FEES

Aside from the costs of starting and running your business, you will then have to bear all the costs of the license. These, in addition to legal obstacles, are often enough to discourage many would-be dispensary owners. In some places, the license fee can exceed tens of thousands of dollars. Add the annual fee to renew your license and it's clear how quickly the money can be sucked out of your wallet.

OBTAINING LICENSES FOR GROWING CANNABIS IN AMERICA, CANADA AND EUROPE

The above is a snapshot of the different factors you will need to consider on a more or less global basis. We will now shed some light on the specific requirements for licensing in America, Canada and Europe, to help you get an idea of how things are in your area.

UNITED STATES

In the United States, laws and regulations for commercial growing vary from state to state, county to county, and even from city to city. So, before you start making plans for opening a dispensary or large-scale cannabis grow, make sure you know the laws and regulations that apply to you.

Licensing fees also vary widely. For example, in Washington state, license fees are only $ 250, with annual fees of $ 1,480. This is a bargain compared to most other states. In Illinois, the registration fee is $ 25,000, with the annual grow license costing $ 100,000. Some states, such as California, Colorado, and Oregon, have variable annual licensing and renewal costs that depend on the size and type of cultivation: indoor or outdoor, number of plants being grown, and so on. In the best cases this can cost you a couple of thousand dollars, but it can go up to tens or hundreds of thousands of dollars just to get and keep your grow license.

CANADA

Canada officially passed the C-45 (Cannabis Act) in October 2018, making it the only G7 country that allows the cultivation and sale of recreational cannabis. This means that cannabis in Canada is federally legal. All aspects of the sale and distribution of cannabis are however under provincial jurisdiction, with different rules for licensing retailers. The Cannabis Legalization and Regulation Branch (CLRB) is responsible for overseeing the licensing process.

Where and how the license is obtained in Canada depends on which province will host the headquarters. For example, in British Columbia it is necessary to obtain a license as a private enterprise from the British Columbia Liquor and Cannabis Regulation Branch (LCRB) by following a detailed application process. In Manitoba, the Manitoba Liquor and Gaming Authority (LGA) issues retail licenses, but individual municipalities can veto the opening of stores in their area.

In Ontario, a license as a dispensary can be obtained by following a detailed application process to be sent to Ontario Cannabis Retail Corporation (OCRC). In Alberta, the application is sent to the Alberta Gaming and Liquor Commission (AGLC).

EUROPE

Unlike Canada and US states where cannabis is legal, all EU member states make possession of cannabis for personal use a criminal offense. However, several countries such as Spain, Italy, the Czech Republic and Belgium have begun to eliminate detention as a penalty for minor offenses.

No government in Europe openly supports the legalization of cannabis for recreational use: the legal cannabis market in Europe exists today only in a medical context. Even dispensaries and coffeeshops in the Netherlands are simply tolerated, as long as they follow strict criteria set by the public authority. This works similar to cannabis clubs in Spain, which are technically private venues, not commercial retail spaces.

Due to the legal status of cannabis in European nations, it is not yet possible to apply for a license to sell recreational cannabis today, although small steps have been taken.

Germany, for example, assigned the first national licenses for medical cannabis cultivation in 2019, although the process has so far been complicated by setbacks and delays. Germany recently restarted the application process, and companies that are eventually selected to legally grow German medical cannabis will have to comply with strict safety requirements and the highest pharmaceutical manufacturing standards.

CANNABUSINESS LICENSE: YOU NEED MONEY, TIME AND ENERGY

If you live in Canada or one of the US states where it is legal you can apply for a license to sell or grow cannabis. This is if you are willing to invest a huge amount of money (and energy, and time) in a very competitive industry where success is far from certain. Here in Europe, things are moving more slowly for aspiring commercial growers. Cannabis is still illegal in the eyes of the law, despite several attempts at decriminalization made here and there. But if the markets where cannabis is already legal teach us anything, it is that things can change quickly.

CHAPTER 8: LIGHT HEMP SHOP IN FRANCHISING

Is it worth opening a light hemp franchise? Are there really good business opportunities in this sector? Or is it a bad investment?

In the guide we will analyze the state of the art of this specific sector, one of the most innovative for those looking for good business opportunities. Cannabis light is liked by many, almost everyone and also allows you to open a business that sells many different products, which can have appeal to many categories of customers.

Let's see together why this could be your next business idea, the one that will be able to lead you into the world of profitable investment, work you like, and business opportunities.

Why cannabis light?

Before going into more specifics, it is more than legitimate to ask why such a sector exists, in fact, the light cannabis franchise, and why it is attracting more and more investors.

While standard cannabis is now on the market almost everywhere in Canada and the US, a little bit all over Europe (except for the Netherlands), there are important restrictions on the marketing of products with a high THC rate.

The problem has been solved by creating hemp species that contain very low percentages and that can be sold freely.

It is not just about food or smoking hemp, but about products that use this extraordinary plant as a raw material, such as oils, creams and incense.

The sector is very diverse and allows everyone to find products suitable for their needs - light cannabis shops have become meeting points for enthusiasts and less enthusiasts and bring home pretty good profits.

A premium product, with high costs and revenues

This is by no means a product for everyone - average prices are over 10 euros per gram, with significant markups for both producers and those who trade the product. This means that those who choose a light hemp franchise can count on a product capable of filling the cash register even with sales volumes that are not exactly big scale.

This particularity of the market must also be taken into consideration with regard to the choice of location: cannabis shops are more than good in selected urban contexts, where those who frequent them are able to spend without too many thoughts.

A growing market for some years now

If the wide margins enjoyed by the products were not enough, it is worth remembering that the cannabis light market has been growing steadily for some years now, which also attracts customers who have never consumed the illegal product.

It is no longer a niche product, but a legitimate product for many customers, with different personal stories, but united by a passion for legal marijuana.

The law is clear: it can be opened and operated without problems

When we talk about legal cannabis and the convenience of opening a franchise or not (or even a shop on your own) it is more than legitimate to worry about the legality of the product.

For a few years, smart shops have been in a gray area, which has led managers to have major problems, which in many cases have led to the closure of businesses.

Today things, at least as regards light cannabis, have definitely changed and there is finally a certain law that protects all operators in the sector:

Marijuana can be sold freely, as long as it has a THC concentration of less than 0.2%;

In any case, between 0.2% and 0.6% are exempt from any penal consequences;

The law is clear and further jurisprudential rulings have helped to define the boundaries of the legality of such a business.

To understand this, today you can open your own light cannabis franchise shop without any consequences, without risking anything, operating like any other entrepreneur.

If you want to sell cannabis light - better go to a good franchise

If you want to sell cannabis light, we advise you to choose a good franchise offer, which guarantees you among other things:

A quality product, which is able to satisfy your customers and to remain within the strict limits set by law;

Intelligent warehouse management, with the right assortments, the possibility of returns and possibly also with the sales account;

A brand known as much as possible: even if there is a premium price to pay, a known brand allows you to operate on the market with greater ease - also avoiding start-up costs in the advertising sector;

By focusing on these characteristics, you will be more than certain to be able to identify a really convenient franchise and that it will give you good support for your entry into the sector and for management once the business is actually started.

CHAPTER 9: LICENSES AND BUREAUCRATIC PROCEDURES IN THE USA

Eleven states in the United States have so far legalized cannabis for non-medical use by adults, with many more ready to follow. With cannabis still federally illegal, a series of natural experiments are taking place, each presenting a different model of how cannabis can be regulated, thus providing important lessons for policymakers looking to pursue similar policies. In this report, we compare regulation across states, taking into account key objectives, including public health and social justice, and consider lessons that can be learned for future policy reform.

The transition from the market to therapeutic use

Cannabis is now legal for medical purposes in most of the United States, so many states have drawn the architecture of their non-medical cannabis distribution system on existing models. Illinois, for example, implemented an "early demand" system for companies already licensed to retail medical cannabis in the area, before sales began in January 2020. In Michigan, the Marijuana Regulatory Agency has made having a state operating license for medical cannabis a requirement to obtain certain types of licenses.

While such strategies simplify the administrative process of developing a new retail market, they also create significant barriers to entry, particularly for small businesses and suppliers based in local communities. The existing medical cannabis production and sales infrastructure therefore does not offer the best platform for non-medical procurement if the goal is to promote local involvement. The investment necessary to start structures oriented to medical production inevitably excludes small producers, even if giving priority to activities active in the therapeutic field allows for a smoother regulatory transition.

Granting of Licenses

Licensing is the key mechanism for regulating sales and checking product availability. States have adopted a number of different licensing systems, leading to different results.

Cannabis licensing in the USA

All states have tried to give municipalities and local authorities some degree of autonomy in regulating non-medical cannabis within their communities: including the flexibility of zoning rules or the option to ban retailers altogether. In California, this has resulted in 76% of cities turning down cannabis shops, leading to criticism that the patchwork of bans is undermining regulatory efforts in tackling the state-level illegal market. States attempt a balance in ensuring access to retail markets by taking into account the concerns of municipalities and have responded in several ways. In Oregon, for example, cities and counties had direct authority until December 2015 to implement local bans if their residents voted at least 55 percent against legalization, although only five cities did.

Taxation

Legal regulation allows you to tax profits from cannabis markets. The collected tax can be spent in various ways in addition to financing the implementation of the regulatory framework, including social projects (if desired). However, it is also a key lever for influencing the retail price.

Some states have tried to allocate revenue (or "mortgage it") for social purposes. In Illinois, 20% of state cannabis taxes goes to basic services to "tackle substance abuse ... prevention and mental health problems" and 2% goes to the Drug Treatment Fund to help with its public education campaign and consequently, analyze the public health impacts of regulation. In Oregon, 20% of the taxes goes directly to the Mental Health Alcoholism and Drug Services Account that provides care for prevention, intervention and treatment of drug abuse and a further 5% goes to the health authority for prevention and of alcohol and drug abuse.

State Excise Other taxes

Washington 37% 7-10% additional state and local sales tax.

Colorado 15% Additional 15% 'special marijuana sales tax' and additional 2.9% state sales tax.

Illinois 10% for THC <35%

25% for THC> 35%

20% on all cannabis infusions

Additional 7% cultivation tax on gross income.

Municipalities and counties can add additional taxes to stores up to 3% and 3.75% respectively.

Nevada 15% off the wholesale price (paid by the grower)

10% on retail

Tax on retail sales at the local rate.

Oregon 17%. Up to 3% additional local taxes.

Massachusetts 10.75%. Additional 6.25% state general sales tax and up to 3% optional local tax.

Maine 10%. Additional 10% sales tax on grower-to-retailer or derivatives producer sales.

California 15%. Growth Fee per ounce of dry produce: $ 9.25 for flowers; $ 2.75 for the leaves or $ 1.29 for the cannabis plant.

Local governments can apply additional taxes.

Michigan 10%. Additional 6% state sales tax.

Alaska Buds: $ 50 per ounce, and Ripe Flowers: $ 15 per ounce.

Abnormal / immature buds and flowers: $ 25 per ounce.

Cuttings: $ 1 per cuttings.

Vermont N / A

PACKAGING, ADVERTISING AND MARKETING

All states have packaging controls, including the definition of various "universal symbology" systems to ensure that it is clear when a product contains cannabis, as well as the inclusion of warnings about potential driving hazards or the need to keep away from children. In some states there are specific restrictions to prevent accidental use by children, which include a ban on the use of characters that children like, such as cartoon characters.

All states require the THC content to be specified on the packaging. All states also require that cannabis be contained in resealable and child resistant packages and in all states, except Oregon, they must be opaque. The degree of uniformity on this issue reflects a certain consensus on the common objectives of regulation, especially in relation to public health and the protection of minors.

Removal from criminal records (expungement)

The moves to regulate represent a radical change in social views on cannabis use; however, previous criminal records remain an enduring stigma that people carry with them. The so-called "expungement", which means the destruction or deletion from the criminal record of an individual's background, allows states to remove this burden from individuals and, to some extent, recognize the errors of previous policy. The expungement is technically different from the "Record sealing", a process according to which the precedent in the criminal record is not canceled, but hidden from the public record and therefore can only be recalled in certain situations.

Status Type of previous penalty removal - Automatic?

California Record sealing Yes

Oregon Record sealing

Individuals can file a motion to request a court order to set aside convictions for now legal conduct. A law in 2020 removed the demand for fees to be paid.

Nevada Record sealing

Individuals can request a court order to set aside convictions for now decriminalized conduct.

Vermont Expungement / Record sealing

Individuals can file a petition requesting Expungement or Sealing from the criminal record if the conduct is no longer prohibited by law or defined as a criminal offense.

Washington Record sealing

The individual can file a request with the court to overturn convictions for minor offenses related to cannabis. An expedited pardon by the Governor is also possible.

Washington State law does not allow expungement, so cancellation is not the same as expungement.

Colorado Record sealing

At the state level, only record sealing is allowed, but in Denver and Boulder, minor offenses related to cannabis no longer punishable (such as possessing less than an ounce of cannabis) can be overruled.

Massachusetts Expungement

The court can order the cancellation of a "crime at the time of registration which at the time of the cancellation is no longer a crime", but an individual petition is required.

Illinois Expungement

The penal system is obliged to automatically delete any possible annotation that is no longer condemned within specific dates. The Governor can grant pardon by authorizing the cancellation for penalties for possession, production, and possession with the purpose of selling up to 30 grams of cannabis. For higher quantities, the subject can file a motion for cancellation to the State Attorney (up to 500gr).

For certain violations

In Maine, a law has been proposed that would oblige "the Department of Public Security to cancel, by July 1, 2020, all criminal recordings related to crime for conduct now authorized by the regulations on the use of marijuana for adults." But the bill was later declared "dead".

The removal of criminal records can be complicated, and administrative and economic barriers can prevent people from deleting their records from the records, even where technically possible. One way to solve this problem is to automate the elements of the process. In California, Bill 1793 requires the Department of Justice to review past convictions related to cannabis to determine all cases that qualify for the withdrawal or revocation of a sentence, revocation and " sealing " or redefinition, by 1 ° July 2020. In this case, record sealing is effective and automatic: the execution of the operation is entirely the responsibility of the Department of Justice, rather than requiring interested parties to submit their applications.

Social equity measures

Legal regulation of cannabis supply offers states the opportunity to begin repairing the harm to individuals and communities disproportionately affected by the cannabis ban. Legal cannabis is a potentially lucrative sector, and proactive measures are needed to ensure that the benefits are not only widely shared, but directed towards the communities that have suffered the most under prohibition. In some (but not all) states, social equity measures have become a key feature of cannabis regulation to ensure market access for disproportionately affected groups.

As companies need a license to produce or sell cannabis, social equity measures can be integrated into license application procedures to promote access for affected individuals disproportionately. In Nevada, "business diversity " (i.e. the presence in the company of people of different ethnic, cultural, social, age and gender, ed) is required and counted when license applications are evaluated, and ends up in the Overall Applicant Scores. In Illinois, up to one-fifth of points in the dispensary license application scoring system are eligible for social equity applicant status. Additional measures to facilitate market access include exemptions and loans. Illinois has proposed a low-interest loan program in areas where prohibition has had a disproportionate impact, with funding of $ 30 million, as well as licensing tax cuts of up to 50 percent. Loan programs also help mitigate financial obstacles to business startups. This is particularly important since the lack of banking services available to cannabis companies (given the ban on banks from having dealings with "illegal" companies at the federal level) has been reported as an "effective blockade for almost everyone," if not rich and well connected, from entering and benefiting from the industry". While loans and tax exemptions are key to promoting early access to the industry, training, technical assistance and mentoring - such as that offered by the Massachusetts Social Equity Program - are key to ensuring long-term success.

Conversely, some states have no social equity schemes at all. Washington state, for example, has been criticized for failing to support minority groups in the cannabis industry. In response, it detailed new proposals to increase business diversity, but it is unclear how practical they are, especially since it is currently not accepting new license applications. The difficulty of retroactively applying equity measures highlights the fundamental importance of putting business diversity and equity at the center of the regulatory framework from the outset.

Lessons learned

The legal regulation of cannabis is still relatively new. We cannot know the full impact until the policies have had time to roll out and the longer-term market readjustments have taken place. In the United States we are seeing a number of approaches, with large differences between states but also a high level of "policy transfer". It is unclear how these approaches will shape the size and pattern of markets in the long term; however, we can already begin to see how different regulatory models lead or facilitate different results. For example, the system shift directly from medical to non-medical retail may exclude smaller operators; allowing the possibility of local prohibition, while creating local democratic accountability, can also create regulatory patchwork; the availability of " expungement " processes can be compromised if these are excessively complicated; and failing to establish proactive measures of social equity from the outset can reinforce inequality in the new market and create an environment in which those most affected by the previous system are excluded from reaping the benefits of change.

The United States is undergoing a revolution in their approach to cannabis. Like all revolutions, however, the results are uncertain. Legal regulation offers a unique opportunity to address the dire injustices that prevent normalization, but it can also transfer financial benefits away from local communities and into the pockets of large corporations. Regulation should not replace one set of inequalities with others. Looking through the experiences of states that have legalized so far, we can see the drift in both directions: corporate dominance and the lack of market access to groups that have been disproportionately impacted by prohibition in some cases, careful efforts to ensure the economic inclusion and addressing historical injustice in others. Getting the best results is often a question of detail: how are licensing systems built in relation to entry costs? What are the systems for handling past convictions? What are the precise rules on marketing and promotion? As we move through high-level debates for change in a world where it is already happening, these details matter. Therefore, while we are still awaiting evidence of some long-term consequences, this report suggests that there are essential considerations that must be part of the regulatory design from the outset if the goals are to be realized - improving public health, protection of the human being, his rights and the promotion of social justice in the best possible way.

CHAPTER 10: THE DISPENSARY FOR MARIJUANA

Do you want to start a medical marijuana dispensary in the United States? If YES, here is a detailed guide on how to obtain a dispensary license in Texas, California, Florida, Michigan, and Maryland. Marijuana is steadily gaining ground in the United States, although it still remains federally illegal. States have now begun to enact laws regulating the marijuana industry. These laws determine who can grow or sell marijuana and under what conditions they can do so. Aside from medical and research purposes, most states have made the affairs of the marijuana dispensary legal. For this reason, many entrepreneurs are now considering owning marijuana dispensaries. To own and operate a marijuana dispensary in the US, you need to obtain a license. The type of license and documentation your marijuana company requires will depend on both the location of your operation and the type of business you are running. This is why you need to do a lot of research before starting. If you are looking for ways to obtain a marijuana dispensary license in the United States, we have listed the states that have legalized marijuana dispensaries. We've also included where you can get these licenses and some of the guidelines you need to follow when applying.

ALASKA

A Detailed Guide to Obtaining a Marijuana Dispensing License in the United States: Alaska.

It has been confirmed that Alaska is one of the states in the United States that allows the use of marijuana, but only for those 21 years of age and older. This state authorizes companies to grow, produce and sell marijuana. If you want to open a marijuana dispensary in Alaska, you need to apply for a license, and this can be done online at the Department of Commerce, Community and Economic Development, MARIJUANA ALCOHOL CONTROL OFFICE. Fingerprints must be submitted with each application. Fingerprint cards cannot be sent electronically to AMCO but physically. Applicants must use an approved agency to obtain their fingerprints. They can also get marijuana growing permits, product manufacturing facilities, testing facilities, retail stores here.

ARIZONA

In Arizona, registered patients can possess and use medical marijuana. Licensed state-owned companies can grow, process, transport and distribute medical marijuana. All marijuana dispensary license applications must be filed online with the Arizona Department of Health Services. The site also lists the requirements for the application. Additionally, Arizona requires all cultivation facilities to be licensed as dispensaries. The Department will first determine if there is a county where there is no dispensary registration certificate. If there is one, then it would be easier to get a license there. All the necessary information about this is available on the website.

ARKANSAS

According to the dispensary licenses in Arkansas, all individuals with legal prescription can possess and use medical marijuana. Licensed state-owned companies can grow, process, transport and distribute medical marijuana.

The Arkansas Medical Marijuana Commission is responsible for the states' medical marijuana program. The commission had established strict guidelines for obtaining a dispensary license and they included: No more than 32 dispensary licenses will be awarded within the "8 dispensary zones" Dispensary location cannot be less than 1,500 feet from a school, one church or kindergarten. No more than 1 license should be issued to any entity. The application fee for dispensary licenses is set at $ 7,500 (half of the application fee will be refunded if the license is not granted). There is a two-tier licensing system for dispensaries: A tier of those dispensaries intending to grow marijuana will be included - a dispensary can choose to grow fifty (50) mature marijuana plants. A second tier will consist of those dispensaries that do not intend to grow marijuana. The applicant must declare their intention to grow or not to grow at the time of submitting the application. Within 7 days of receiving the commission's written notice of the selection, the selected applicant must submit a licensing fee of $ 15,000.00 in cash or certified funds, as well as a performance bond in the amount of $ 100,000.00.

CALIFORNIA

In California, the Bureau issues temporary cannabis control marijuana dispensary licenses, cannabis growing licenses of CDFA, and cannabis safety branch produced by CDPH. Growers, producers, retailers, distributors, micro-enterprises, test labs and event organizers can apply for their licenses from these offices. Applications for annual licenses will be accepted through an online licensing system - the Manufactured Cannabis Licensing System (MLCS).

This application will require information about the company, owners, financial interest holders and operating premises, as well as the description of procedures for waste disposal, inventory and quality control, transportation and safety. More information can be obtained on the California cannabis portal.

COLORADO

If you intend to own a Colorado Retail Marijuana Business you should also visit the Colorado Marijuana Owners and Investors page. Licenses are available for both medical and recreational marijuana. The guidelines for obtaining a retail license in Colorado include that applicants must apply to the state for a retail license before selling marijuana, must confirm that the local authority in which it is planned to operate allows retail marijuana stores to operate within their jurisdiction. Applicants must be resident in the state of the Colorado for at least 2 years before applying for a license. Number of retail stores licenses are limited by the local government Applicant must submit a non-refundable application fee of $ 4,500.

CONNECTICUT

In Connecticut, all qualified patients with legal prescriptions can be in possession of marijuana and licensed state companies can grow, process, transport and dispense marijuana. The Connecticut Department of Consumer Protection is responsible for the States Medical Marijuana

Program, and all applications are filed there. from authorized manufacturers, to patients and qualified healthcare professionals. During the application, there is a non-refundable application fee of $ 1,000 payable at the time of application and a non-refundable application fee of $ 5,000. All marijuana businesses must be located at least 300 meters from places used primarily for religious worship, public or private school, convent, charitable institution, supported by public or private funds, hospital or veterans' home or from any military camp or establishment.

Documentation that must be provided when submitting the application; Personal Information, Latest Employment Information, Dispensing Facility Information, Licenses, Permits, and Records, Professional History, Criminal Actions, Photo Identification, (Passport-sized Photograph and Copy of Valid Government-Issued ID) License Fee, Initial Tuition Fee: $ 1,000 [non-refundable] Registration fee: $ 5,000 [non-refundable] Renewal fee: $ 5,000 [non-refundable] License and renewal fees: $ 100 each Registration / renewal of dispensary technician and dispensary staff: $ 50 Registration / Dispensary Facility Supporter Renewal: $ 100 Dispensary Name Change Application: $ 100 Dispensary Facility Manager Change: $ 50 Location Change or Expansion Application: $ 1,000 [plus $ 1,500 if approved], Application of physical, non-cosmetic modification of the structure [other than expansion]: $ 500. Questions and materials support must be delivered by hand according to the instructions in the application request, along with an application fee of $ 25,000.

DELAWARE

In Delaware, all persons with legal prescriptions can possess and use medical marijuana. Licensed state companies can grow, process, transport and distribute medical marijuana. The Department of Health is responsible for issuing this license through the medical marijuana program. The state only grants licenses to compassion centers and has strict guidelines for opening these centers.

They include; a compassion center must be run on a non-profit basis. A compassion center must not be located less than 300 meters from the property line of an existing public or private school. New applicants for a Compassion Center license will only be accepted during an open application period announced by the Department. A non-refundable application fee, made payable to the Division of Public Health, Medical Marijuana Program, in the amount of $ 5,000 will be required at the time of application. There is currently one compassion center and another opening soon.

FLORIDA

Licensed distribution organizations are licensed to cultivate the process and dispense medical marijuana. These are the only companies in Florida licensed to distribute medical marijuana to qualified patients and legal representatives. The Office of Medical Marijuana Use (a division of the Florida Department of Health) is responsible for drafting and enforcing the department's rules and licensing activities for dispensing, processing and growing medical marijuana. The Office is not currently accepting applications for medical marijuana treatment centers.

HAWAII

In Hawaii, anyone with a legal prescription can possess and use medical marijuana. Licensed state-owned companies can grow, process, transport and distribute medical marijuana. The Hawaii Department of Health Medical Cannabis Dispensing Program is responsible for licensing. The dispensary licensing guidelines for Hawaii are therefore; Non-refundable application fee of $ 5,000. An application must state that applicants have resources in the amount of $ 1,000,000, plus a minimum of $ 100,000 for each retail location the applicant wishes to operate. A distributor licensee can manage up to two retail distribution points. If an applicant intends to operate two retail distribution points, the total money an applicant must have in reserve at the time of application is $ 1,200,000. Applicants can apply for more than one license, but only one license can be issued. If an applicant is entitled to more than one license, they will need to choose the county in which they want to operate a dispensary.

ILLINOIS

In Illinois, all individuals with a legal prescription can possess and use medical marijuana. Licensed state-owned companies can grow, process, transport, and distribute medical marijuana. The Illinois Department of Financial and Professional Regulation is responsible for licensing dispensaries. At the moment they do not issue any licenses.

IOWA

In Iowa, qualified patients can use, possess and access low-THC cannabis oil. The production, delivery, transportation and dispensing of cannabidiol are permitted by authorized license holders. The Iowa Department of Public Health is authorized to select and license five medical cannabidiol dispensaries in Iowa. Dispensaries selected through the competitive process will obtain licenses from the department to legally provide medical cannabidiol to patients and primary caregivers with valid medical cannabidiol registration cards. Licensed dispensaries must be ready to begin providing medical cannabidiol by December 1, 2018. The law sets the non-refundable application fee for a dispensary license at $ 5,000.

LOUISIANA

In Louisiana, people with a legal recommendation from their doctor can be in possession of medical marijuana, and licensed state pharmacies can dispense medical marijuana.

The Louisiana Board of Pharmacy is responsible for licensing. The state has a number of laws for opening dispensaries, and one of their laws limits the number of licenses to be distributed to 10. Others include; Only existing pharmacies are allowed to dispense medical marijuana a single manufacturing facility will be responsible for growing, which one or both Louisiana State University and Southern University have the first right of refusal to grow medical marijuana collaboratively or separately. No more than 10 pharmacies can obtain licenses to dispense marijuana within the state. In the state, pharmacists can only dispense marijuana grown in state universities. Those wishing to prescribe medical marijuana in Louisiana must pay an application fee of $ 5,000 in addition to a licensing fee of $ 150 to become one of the 10 marijuana pharmacists in the state. The $ 5,000 application fee is non-refundable and only applies to marijuana pharmacies, not regular drug stores.

MAINE

In Maine, all individuals can be in possession of marijuana. The state is currently working on rules to establish a system for state-owned companies licensed to grow, process, transport and distribute recreational marijuana. License applicants must be at least 21 years old, citizens of Maine and have a verifiable SSN. Their businesses must be a corporation, association, LLC or organization. If the applicant is a corporation, all board members must meet the criteria above. Also, criminal convictions punishable by five years or more may automatically disqualify candidates, provided they have not elapsed 10 years or more since have occurred. Licenses for dispensaries are provided but are rarely available. The retail marijuana store license is as follows: license fee of $ 250- $ 2,500; non-refundable application fee of $ 10- $ 250

MARYLAND

In Maryland, all individuals with a prescription can possess and use medical marijuana. The Maryland Medical Cannabis Commission is responsible for developing policies, procedures and regulations for the use of medical marijuana, as well as licensing. It has issued medical cannabis dispensary pre-approvals to 102 companies, with 22 approved and the others in phase 2 of the approval process.

MASSACHUSETTS

In Massachusetts, people over the age of 21 can own up to one ounce of marijuana, keep up to 10 ounces of marijuana at home, and grow up to six plants. Licensed state-owned enterprises can grow, produce, distribute and sell marijuana. All information on licensing marijuana establishments through the Cannabis Control Commission must be obtained on the Commission's website Applicants are required to pay $ 1,500 for the intent request and $ 30,000 for the management profile application and Operations Applications can be submitted by mail to the Cannabis Control Commission, 101 Federal Street, 13th Floor, Boston, MA 02110. In order to obtain a license in accordance with the Adult Use of Marijuana Act passed in 2016, you must apply for the Cannabis Control Commission.

MICHIGAN

In Michigan, people 21 years of age and older can possess and use marijuana. Licensed state-owned companies can grow, process, transport and distribute marijuana. Here are some of the requirements to apply for a marijuana dispensary license in Michigan; An applicant may have to pay a fee to their local city / municipality of up to $ 5,000 and a non-refundable state application fee of $ 6,000. The applicant, if an individual, must have been a resident of the State of Michigan for a continuous period of 2 years.

This requirement does not apply after June 30, 2018. The applicant is ineligible if he has been convicted or released from incarceration under the laws of this state, any other state of the United States (federal law) within the past 10 years or has been convicted of a controlled substance-related crime within the past 10 years. The applicant is ineligible if he has been convicted of a crime involving a controlled substance, theft, dishonesty or fraud in any state within the past 5 years. Must apply for a procurement center license with the local city and state before selling marijuana and marijuana products. The Regulations. of the Office of Medical Marijuana is responsible for the supervision of medical marijuana and is composed of the Medical Marijuana Program and the Facility Licensing Division. The Licensing and Regulatory Affairs Department is currently accepting applications for growers, processors, transporters, procurement centers and safety compliance facilities.

MINNESOTA

Minnesota On May 29, 2014, Governor Mark Dayton signed a bipartisan medical marijuana proposal that was drafted by a House and Senate conference committee, making Minnesota the 22nd state to exempt some sufferers and their caregivers from penalty for using marijuana with a medical certification. Licenses for marijuana companies are not available. The Department of Health has selected two companies as registered marijuana producers and distributors.

The state has 8 dispensaries, which are called centers for cannabis patients. A non-refundable application fee of $ 20,000 is required for registration.

MONTANA

In Montana, only registered cardholders are allowed to own and use marijuana. The Montana Department of Public Health and Human Services is in charge of the States Medical

Marijuana Program. Questions for the provider, test lab, and dispensary licenses are available periodically. The proposed test rooms or laboratories may not be less than 150 meters away and on the same street as a building used exclusively as a church, synagogue or other place of worship or secondary school or post-school other than a commercially operated school.

NEVADA

Nevada legalized medical marijuana on November 7, 2000, when 65% of the population voted yes on question 9. The Nevada Tax Department is responsible for licensing and regulating retail marijuana businesses and the state medical marijuana program. As of November 2018, only holders of existing medical marijuana establishment certificates can apply for a retail marijuana establishment license. Fees you may incur in attempting to open a dispensary in Nevada: Medical Marijuana Institution Registration Certificate: $ 5,000 [non-refundable, applies to all of the following in addition to lower fees]; Pantry Registration Certificate: $ 30,000; Pantry Certificate Renewal: $ 5,000; Growing Facility Registration Certificate: $ 3,000; Growing Facility Certificate Renewal: $ 1,000; Facility producing edible marijuana or marijuana products - Certificate of Registration: $ 3,000; Edible Manufacturing Facility Certificate Renewal: $ 1,000; MM Agent Registration Card: $ 75; Card Renewal Agent: $ 75; Certificate of Registration of independent testing laboratory: $ 5,000; Renewal of certain Independent Testing Lab Fee: $ 3,000; Some guidelines include that applicants must submit a non-refundable application fee of $ 5,000.

They must show proof of the amount of taxes paid or other beneficial financial contributions paid to this State or its political subdivisions over the past 5 years by the applicant or persons who purport to be owners, officers or board members of the proposed marijuana business. Again, the retail marijuana store must be at least 300m from a public or private school and 30m from a community facility. Not more than 80 licenses issued in a county with a population of less than 700,000. No more than 20 licenses issued in a county with a population of less than 700,000 but more than 100,000. Not more than 4 licenses issued in a county with a population of less than 100,000 but greater than 55,000. No more than 2 licenses issued in a county with a population of less than 55,000.

NEW HAMPSHIRE

In New Hampshire, anyone with a legal prescription can possess and use medical marijuana. The New Hampshire Department of Health and Human Services is responsible for managing the cannabis therapeutic program. The Department established New Hampshire's terms for 4 Alternative Treatment Center (ATC) dispensaries. These centers are the only ones needed to own, grow, acquire, deliver, produce, transfer, supply, sell, distribute and transport cannabis and other related supplies, as well as provide educational materials for both eligible patients and other alternative treatment centers.

NEW JERSEY

In New Jersey, anyone with a legal prescription can be in possession of marijuana, and licensed state companies can grow, process, transport, and dispense marijuana. The New Jersey Department of Health is in charge of the States Medicinal Marijuana Program. State licensing firms called Alternative Treatment Centers (ATCs) for the production and distribution of medical marijuana. Six ATCs have been licensed. Once the initial six are opened, the state will evaluate the program and determine whether or not expansion is needed. At present, however, the state does not license any medical marijuana business.

NEW MEXICO

The New Mexico Department of Health is responsible for overseeing the medical cannabis program. To produce, distribute and distribute medical marijuana, you must be a licensed nonprofit producer (LNPP). A non-profit producer operates a facility and, at any one time, is limited to a combined total of no more than 450 mature female male plants, seedlings, and plants.

In this period, LNPP application is closed and the department is not currently accepting applications for medical marijuana production and distribution. Currently, there are 50 licensed cannabis dispensaries in New Mexico with an estimated 50,954 registered patients. At the end of 2016, the cannabis market in New Mexico exceeded $ 50.6 million.

NEW YORK

The New York Department of Health is in charge of its medical marijuana program. Only registered organizations can produce and distribute medical marijuana. The

Department began accepting applications for registration as a registered organization on April 27, 2015. Each applicant was required to submit two fees with their application: a non-refundable application fee in the amount of $ 10,000 and a registration fee for an amount of $ 200,000. The $ 200,000 registration fee is to be refunded to the applicant only if the applicant has not been issued a registration. The Department does not currently accept applications to become a registered organization.

NORTH DAKOTA

The Division of Medical Marijuana (part of the North Dakota Department of Health) is in charge of the state's medical marijuana program. Compassion centers are dispensaries or facilities for marijuana growers / producers. The application period for compassion centers is currently closed. Some of their application guidelines include that: Compassion centers are required to maintain adequate security, including well-lit entrances, an alarm system that contacts law enforcement, and video surveillance. They may not be within 1,000 feet of a school and will be subject to inspections and other regulations.

There is a $ 5,000 non-refundable application fee to submit a proposal (application) and a $ 90,000 certification fee upon issuance of the license. Compassion Center licenses will be granted on the basis of a merit-based application procedure, which will consider: the suitability of the proposed venue; the character and competence of applicants in related fields; proposed center plans, including those related to record keeping, security, personnel and training, to prevent diversion. Every staff member of a compassion center must apply for and obtain a registry photo ID card. They must be at least 21 years of age and must not have been convicted of a crime of barred crime or a recent drug. Compassion Center membership fee is non-refundable.

OHIO

Under new regulations, enacted September 8, 2016, Ohio is ready to welcome medical marijuana businesses. While the state has already licensed a limited number of growers, dispensaries, and other businesses, it can issue multiple licenses as needed to meet demand.

OKLAHOMA

With the death of SQ 788 in June 2018, Oklahoma became the 30th state in the United States to legalize medical marijuana. Oklahoma residents over the age of 18 with a valid medical recommendation can apply for a license for a medical marijuana patient. If approved, they can purchase medical marijuana from licensed dispensaries across the state. Dispensaries in Oklahoma must be located at least 300 meters from a public or private school. This is measured by a straight line (the shortest distance) from the dispensary property line to any school entrance.

The Oklahoma State Department of Health is responsible for approving licenses and they have some application criteria which include; The applicant must be twenty five (25) years of age or older; Any applicant, presenting himself as an individual, must exhibit residence in the state of Oklahoma; All applicant entities must demonstrate that all members, officers and board members are resident in Oklahoma; An applicant entity can show ownership of non-Oklahoma residents, but this percentage cannot exceed 25% (25%). All applicant persons or entities must be registered to conduct business in the state of Oklahoma; All applicants must disclose all ownership; Applicant (s) with only convictions for nonviolent crimes in the past two (2) years, any other felony convictions over five (5) years, inmates or any other person currently incarcerated are not eligible for a medical marijuana dispensary license.

OREGON

In 2013, Oregon House Bill 3460 became law, allowing medical marijuana dispensaries to be registered. The legislation went into effect on March 1, 2014. Licenses are mandatory and available for medical and recreational marijuana companies. The state requires separate licenses and registrations for growers and dispensary operators. The Oregon Liquor Control Commission (OLCC) license accepts applications for marijuana licenses. The application fee is usually $ 3,500 and the application fee is $ 500. There is also an annual tracking system fee of $ 480. Each applicant must also pay $ 35 for a background check. Furthermore, there will be a huge capital of up to $ 500,000 to open a new cannabis dispensary.

RHODE ISLAND

According to state law of Rhode Island, cannabis businesses such as dispensaries, must be defined compassion centers. A compassion center in the state of Rhode Island can do any of the following: growing, processing, transporting, as well as selling cannabis to all registered patients and registered primary care providers. Applications can only be submitted during an open application period announced by the state if necessary.

The state has 3 licensed compassion centers currently in operation. Each application for a compassion center must include: A non-refundable application fee paid to the department in the amount of two hundred and fifty dollars ($ 250); The proposed legal name and proposed incorporation of the compassion center; the proposed physical address of the compassion center, if a specific address has been determined or, if not, the general location where it would be located. This may include a second location for medical marijuana cultivation; A description of the closed facility that would be used in the cultivation of marijuana; The name, address, and date of birth of each principal officer and board member of the compassion center; Proposed safety and security measures that include at least one security alert system for each location, planned measures to deter and prevent unauthorized entry into areas containing marijuana and theft of marijuana, as well as a draft, instruction manual for employees which includes security policies, personal safety and security procedures, and crime prevention techniques; and proposed procedures to ensure accurate record keeping.

TENNESSEE

In 2014 the state approved SB 2531, a limited medical bill for cannabis, which allows the use of cannabis oil containing CBAAD as part of the Aa clinical research study on its effects on patients with seizure disorders. Tennessee Tech has the opportunity to grow, process and distribute CBD. In

Tennessee, qualified patients can own and use CBD extracts. Current law does not provide for a state-regulated dispensary system.

TEXAS

In Texas, only clinically qualified people are allowed to own or use CBD oil. Licensed state-owned companies can brew, grow and process low-THC marijuana.

The Texas Department of Public Safety (DPS) issues the license. The license will authorize organizations to cultivate the process and dispense low-THC cannabis to prescribed patients. The department under the state bill is required to license only three donor organizations, and these organizations have already been licensed. For now, the state is not receiving applications.

UTAH

In Utah, qualified registered patients can possess and use medical marijuana. Authorized state agencies can grow, process and distribute medical marijuana. The Utah Department of Health is responsible for licensing. The applicant will need an operational plan that includes operational procedures that comply with the law; Including financial statements showing that the applicant has a minimum of $ 500,000 in liquid assets available to each cannabis growing facility for which the person applies, or a minimum of $ 100,000 in liquid assets available to each processing facility, cannabis or independent cannabis testing laboratory for which the person applies.

VERMONT

The Department of Public Safety is responsible for the marijuana registry and issues dispensary registration certificates. The Department has issued 4 dispensary registration certificates and 1 conditional certificate. The Department plans to announce an application period for a sixth dispensary once the number of registered patients reaches 7,000. Currently, dispensaries are the only types of licensed marijuana companies in Vermont. Licensees can run two dispensaries with the same license. It is advisable to understand state regulations and also to treat the marijuana business in line with local laws. Application fees are as follows: $ 2,500 for dispensary application; $ 50 for caregiver enrollment application. Licensing fees include: $ 20,000 Initial Waiver Registration Fee; $ 25,000 Renewal Waiver Registration Fee.

WASHINGTON

In 2012, Washington became the first US state to legalize the recreational use of cannabis after more than a decade of medical legalization. With the demise of Initiative 502, adults over the age of 21 were legally allowed to purchase and own cannabis products from licensed distributors. The Washington State Liquor and Cannabis Board is responsible for licensing marijuana; however, it is not currently accepting license requests.

Washington DC. While it is legal to use marijuana recreationally, there are no businesses that sell marijuana for recreational use. The DC Department of Health has a medical marijuana program, but is not currently accepting applications for medical marijuana facilities.

WISCONSIN

In Wisconsin, qualified patients can own and use CBD extracts. State-licensed doctors and pharmacies can dispense CBD extracts to patients. The state of Wisconsin is not currently accepting applications for marijuana companies. West Virginia Governor Jim Justice signed Senate Bill 386, known as the Medical Cannabis Act, on April 20, 2017, making the medicinal use of marijuana legal for qualified patients in West Virginia. Patients will be able to obtain medical cannabis in the following forms: pill, oil, topical forms including gels, creams or ointments, a medically appropriate form for administration by vaporization or nebulization, tincture, liquid or dermal patch. The state intends to issue around 30 dispensary permits to individuals. Individuals wishing to obtain a West Virginia dispensing permit must submit an application that includes the following: Verification of all principal, operator, financier, or employee of a medical cannabis grower / processor or distributor; a description of your responsibilities as a principal, operator, financier or employee; any releases required to obtain information from government agencies, employers and other organizations; a criminal background check; details of any license, permit or other similar authorization obtained in another jurisdiction, including any suspension, revocation or regulation in that jurisdiction; a description of the business activities in which it intends to engage as a medical cannabis organization; application for grant permit will require specific business plans. A statement that the applicant: has a good moral character; possesses the ability to quickly obtain the right to use sufficient land, buildings and other premises and equipment to properly carry out the activity described in the application and any proposed location for a facility; is able to maintain effective security and control to prevent diversion, abuse and other illegal conduct related to medical cannabis; is able to comply with all applicable state laws and regulations relating to the activities in which the applicant intends to engage under this act. Name, residential address and title of each lender and principal of the applicant. Any other information requested by the Office of Public Health States without laws on the use of marijuana for medical or recreational use.

States that currently prohibit the use of marijuana or severely restrict its use include: Alabama Georgia Idaho Indiana Kansas Kentucky Mississippi Nebraska New Hampshire North Carolina South Carolina South Dakota Wyoming

CHAPTER 11: OPENING A DISPENSARY

The recent legalization of marijuana in several states was an unprecedented process. By legitimizing both recreational and medical marijuana, states have opened up a new industry, one that people are clamoring to take advantage of.

We spoke to two dispensary owners from pioneering states: Mitch Woolhiser, owner of the Northern Lights Cannabis company in Denver, Colorado, and Lincoln Fish, CEO of OutCo Labs, which runs the Collective Outliers dispensary in San Diego, California. While the details of their experiences are very different, their general attitude was similar: opening a dispensary is not for the faint of heart. It is a job that takes a lot of hard work and time before it becomes profitable.

"It's one of the hardest things you can do," says Mitch Woolhiser. "It can't just be this fun thing. It has to be taken seriously." In addition to requiring a lot of effort, opening a clinic requires careful compliance with laws and regulations, as well as a large amount of start-up capital. "You won't make any money if you don't follow these rules," says Lincoln Fish. "It's an expensive business to run."

But if hard work, cash up front and bureaucratic red tape don't put you off, opening a dispensary is an opportunity for you to be a pioneer in what will soon be a huge, national industry. Marijuana Business Daily estimates revenue generated by dispensaries and retail stores to reach between $ 6.5 and $ 8 billion by 2019.

"It's still on the ground floor entirely, considering the federal lawlessness of it," Mitch says. "It's still a good time to get in."

STEP 1: ASSESS YOUR COMMITMENT AND ELIGIBILITY

Lincoln Fish moved into the medical marijuana industry to challenge hypocrisy.

"I was with a lot of people. I thought, 'These are drugs, this is bad,' " Lincoln says. "Then you start to realize how much hypocrisy surrounds marijuana. Alcohol and tobacco are much more harmful and much more addictive. Schedule 1 Narcotics by legal definition are highly addictive, prove to have no medicinal benefits, and can be harmful to lethality. Alcohol and tobacco meet all three of these requirements and marijuana does not meet any of them. "

Mitch Woolhiser saw a magnificent and unusual business opportunity in the budding marijuana industry in 2010. "This is something that, as a businessman, you can do almost revolutionary," he says. "It's the chance of a lifetime. What product suddenly becomes legal when it hasn't been for a long time? Not since the alcohol prohibition has such a thing happened and it probably won't happen again in my life."

But Mitch and Lincoln warn against opening a dispensary just for financial gain. "If the only reason you're dealing with this is money, you're not going to have fun," Mitch says. "It's not a get-rich-quick scheme. It's a long game. You have to have something extra to motivate yourself."

It is also important to recognize that background checks are often required, not only for a dispensary owner, but also for investors and employees. If you have a criminal background, you may not be eligible to open a dispensary.

Also, if medical marijuana isn't legalized in your state, any dispensary could be closed by the federal government. If there are no existing laws or regulations in your area, opening a dispensary is probably not a good idea. "If the city or county hasn't gone through anything, the state's default position is that there's nothing legal there," Lincoln says. "You have to be very careful. This could be a problem. You could be turned off."

Considering the money spent to open a dispensary, trying to run one illegally is not worth the risk.

STEP 2: DO YOUR RESEARCH

The dispensary business is full of laws and regulations. To be successful as a dispensary owner, you need to understand not only the existing laws on growing and selling marijuana, but also the proposed laws and changes that will come into effect in the coming years.

Lincoln Fish recommends reading Cole's Memorandum, which provides guidance to US state lawyers on how to prioritize the enforcement of marijuana laws. If you are in California, he also recommends that you read Proposition 215 and Proposition 420.

"In most cities and counties, it's very easy to study and see what the legislation is," says Lincoln. "Either it's banned altogether, [or] if it's not, they've already issued ordinances and guidance."

The National Organization for the Reform of Marijuana Laws, or NORML, has a database of detailed marijuana laws and sanctions for every state in the U.S. These tables from the National Conference of State Legislature are also helpful.

"There are a lot of rules to follow and I highly recommend that people get help right from the start: a lawyer and a CPA attorney," says Lincoln. This will help you comply with the law and access permissions and licenses. NORML has a database of lawyers from all over the United States who specialize in the marijuana industry.

Both Mitch and Lincoln recommend a thorough study of US 280E, a deceptive tax code that can bring dispensary owners down, particularly on the budget.

"If you're dealing with a Schedule I narcotic, which is marijuana, you can only deduct the cost of the goods sold from your income before you do your taxes," Lincoln explains. "Suppose you buy the product for $ 500, put it on the shelf, sell it for $ 1000. You would have to pay taxes on the profit of $ 500 before you can pay the rent, the employees, and so on. What's happening to many dispensaries is that they are driving themselves crazy with huge taxes. This is another reason why opening a dispensary is not necessarily as profitable as people think. "

STEP 3: FIND A RENTAL PROPERTY

"The key is really just to find a compliant property," says Lincoln. In San Diego, a compliant property has many requirements: "To be a compliant property, it must be more than 1,000 feet from a church, 1,000 feet from a school, 1,000 feet from a residential area, and 1,000 feet from another compliant property, "says Lincoln. "There's an online map showing all San Diego County compliant properties."

It is important to remember that due to the ever-changing environment of the marijuana industry, a property that is now compliant may not be in two years. "Make sure when you access a property that it will be consistent with the new laws that come into effect next two years, " says Lincoln. "Make sure you don't open one and close it because they clash with the new laws."

Compliant property means different things in different places, and even if you find a compliant property, you need to be honest with the landlord about your plans to open a dispensary there, and they may not be supportive. Mitch Woolhiser took care of this while looking for space for his dispensary in 2010. "Some owners just didn't want to take care of it and still won't," Mitch says. "Some of these are due to federal lawlessness and the liability they may have."

Owners are sometimes under pressure from law enforcement. Mother Earth Collective, which used to operate in the space that is now Outliers Collective in San Diego, was indirectly forced out by the DEA. "The DEA sent letters to homeowners across the country and said, 'Hey, if we decide to get off on these guys, you can be responsible if you're renting them.' The landlord threw them out and the collective shut down." Lincoln explains.

When looking for a place to open your practice, also consider whether it is convenient for potential clients. "For planning purposes, location is the most important thing on the business side," says Mitch. "People come to you because you are a destination or because you are convenient." Identifying a target market can help you choose a good location for your store.

It is also important that most, if not all members of your community (even non-users who will not be your customers) are comfortable with a dispensary in their area. If your county or city has had proposals to vote on marijuana laws, Mitch recommends accessing the ballot results for any area where you are considering a property.

"In Colorado, in 2012 we voted on Amendment 64, which is the recreational law, " he says. "I visited the Secretary of State's website and got the election results for Edgewater [where the Northern Lights Cannabis Company is located]. In Edgewater it went up to 70%. Any other community, you can find out that information too. You can find out about the results of these questions and decide, on the basis of this information, whether the community will be welcoming or not. "

STEP 4: WRITE A BUSINESS PLAN

When an industry is saturated in the way the medical marijuana industry is, it's all the more important to appear professional and prepared with a solid business plan.

Mitch, who used Bplans to write his dispensary business plan in 2010, says a business plan can separate you from the crowd. "Write a business plan, " he says. "There are a lot of people who get involved in this business and they're not very serious. Understand what you are getting into and don't just listen to someone who is high in the sky."

Access capital

Any good business plan will start with how to access capital, which is one of the most challenging parts of the marijuana industry.

"The barriers to entry are still quite high," says Mitch. "It's going to take a lot more money than it used to. We got in with about fifty thousand dollars and some credit cards. Now, you wouldn't be able to introduce it without at least half a million because of the regulations. Also, because there is a lot of competition. "

Due to the federal illegality of marijuana, it is not possible to obtain a bank loan for a dispensary. Lincoln recommends sticking to personal funds for your starting capital. "You are better off now that you really focus on angelic investors, friends and family to get to the point where you can acquire a property," says Lincoln. "Many investors won't talk to you until you have a lot of pieces under your belt. If you have compliant ownership, it gets easier."

Determine your budget

Another consideration in your business plan is a clear and concise budget.

"You have to create a budget and take 280E into account, Lincoln says." You won't be able to do it with little money. You have to be prepared for it to grow slowly. "

Consult wholesalers in your area to find out the cost of the products. "For the business plan itself, you need to know the costs in regards to the cost of getting the product," says Mitch.

In addition to product costs, there are other considerations for your budget:

- Cost of rental
- Cost of the license
- Cost of the license application
- Salary of the employees
- Transport and storage of the product
- Safety

Competition search

In addition to knowing the licensed competition in your area, opening a dispensary requires thinking about another competitive demographic that presents more challenges: unlicensed operators.

"Understand the landscape of unlicensed competition in that area," says Lincoln. "What is law enforcement doing about it or planning to do? The truth is that unlicensed people are allowed to ramp up. Law enforcement is working to shut them down, but it's not a high priority because they cannot get any sentences ".

Search local publications for pantry ads, both home and delivery. This will give you an idea of the unlicensed operators in your area. Furthermore, the search will focus on unauthorized operations in your area. Are unauthorized dispensaries allowed to function freely, or are law enforcement agencies working to get rid of them? This will be good information to inform your business plan.

"It is very difficult to build a patient base when there are nearby people who are open 24/7, which you won't be able to do, who aren't paying taxes or social security for their employees, they're not paying federal taxes, "Lincoln says. "This will kill you. You have to play by the rules and they don't."

Conduct market research

Your business plan offers you an important opportunity to identify your customers. This will help inform your dispensary's marketing and pricing strategy. "Know your market," Lincoln says. "You know your demographics and psychographics. Is there a consumer demand? Where is it? That will also determine some of your prices."

STEP 5: GET A LICENSE

Getting a license to open a medical marijuana dispensary is usually difficult and expensive. "I've known people who spent up to three or four thousand dollars in legal fees to get their license," says Lincoln. For example, in Colorado, the registration fee for a medical marijuana dispensary can cost up to $ 15,000.

"Be prepared to spend a lot of time on compliance and have a lot of resources for it," says Mitch. "A lot of consolidation has gone on here because a lot of small operations can't keep up with compliance. It's a full-time job."

Take a look at the retail and medical marijuana license application process in Colorado to get an idea of what your application process might look like.

STEP 6: GET PRODUCT

Getting good product for your marijuana dispensary, and making sure you do so legally, will be a central part of opening a successful dispensary. Many dispensaries grow their own marijuana, and in some states this is mandatory.

Mitch Woolhiser has his own grow facility for the Northern Lights Cannabis Company and says it should be on the horizon for every dispensary owner.

"First open a retail facility and then have an eye on your grow facility," he says. "Get your sales off the ground with wholesale products. I'd recommend it."

Opening a dispensary doesn't mean you have to sell marijuana in its typical form. Many patients prefer edibles, oils, tannins and concentrates. Mitch says vendors of these forms of marijuana are easy to find and bargain with. "When it comes to edibles and concentrates, these companies have sales forces," he says. "Just reach out to them and make contact."

STEP 7: MARKET YOUR DISPENSARY

Decide what your competitive dispensary does and sell it.

"You can compete on price or other things, and I chose other things," says Mitch. "We try to be more boutique. For us, ask all the questions, smell and look at each type before deciding which one to buy. Create more of a unique shopping experience."

The Outliers collective is also involved in advertising to a more mature audience. "We are looking for long-term customers who come to us because they want service, quality and consistency," says Lincoln. "We want to spread the word

113 | P a g .

to a different type of patient, people who care about all the things a licensed place represents."

Your target market will inform some of your marketing choices, but Lincoln says there are a few necessities for marketing your new dispensary. "You have to be on Weed Maps and Leafly, " he says. Weed Maps and Leafly are applications that allow patients to search for dispensaries in their area. Lincoln also uses some magazine advertisements and has a billboard on California State Route 67.

Mitch recommends marketing through social media accounts like Instagram, encouraging customers to give reviews on Google and keeping your website up to date with the correct SEO strategies.

It is also important to check your dispensary's marketing regulations. There are many methods Mitch can't use in Colorado: "You can't advertise on radio, TV, billboards," he says. "There are a lot of restrictions. You can't market to out-of-state people. You can't advertise pop-up."

Mitch and Lincoln both use loyalty programs that help market their dispensaries by word of mouth. A program that offers customers store credit when they refer a new customer, such as the Outliers Collective Jane Dough program, will expand your customer base.

STAY INFORMED

With this information you have a good chance of opening a successful, profitable dispensary program.

Lincoln Fish encourages those with the right motivation to enter the relatively new medical marijuana industry: "I'd like to see more responsible and credible people come into our space and open dispensaries and do a good job with it, " he says. "The more we do to show the general public how important and how responsible we can be and how much good can be done, the more we will get public opinion on our side."

With marijuana legislation changing often, it's important to keep up with new information even after you've opened your dispensary to ensure you are operating safely and legally.

CHAPTER 12: HOW MUCH DOES IT COST AND HOW TO OPEN A CANNABIS SHOP IN ITALY?

Following the approval of law 242 of 2016 which protects and encourages the cultivation and processing of hemp, the cannabis market in Italy has seen thousands of companies "flourish" with not a few satisfactions. In fact, opening a cannabis shop can become a very profitable business and can make you good money. Anyone over 18 can become an entrepreneur in the hemp market.

There are basically three ways to open a cannabis shop:

- In autonomy (from scratch)
- In franchising
- Intermediate formula

1) Open a shop selling legal hemp products from scratch.

This is certainly the most complicated way but it can give various satisfactions to an entrepreneur. There is nothing of your company, you will have to create it from scratch, step by step.

You will therefore need to:

- do a market research

- draw up a business plan with objectives and forecasts for the return on investment (ROI)

Finding the funds to invest

Open a VAT number by creating a customized company (sole proprietorship or company) with the help of an accountant

- ✓ Find the right place where the shop will be
- ✓ Renovate or furnish it to make it functional for your purpose
- ✓ Find a name
- ✓ Create the brand
- ✓ Create a corporate image and a marketing strategy
- ✓ Search and compare suppliers
- ✓ Choose and buy products to resell
- ✓ Investing in communication and advertising to promote the brand

The cost to open your own hemp products retail shop from scratch ranges from approximately € 30,000 to € 50,000.

Pros:

- Autonomous choice of name, products and suppliers.
- Total independence of the company
- Greater profits should the company grow over the years

Versus:

- High opening costs
- Greater business risks

Greater efforts in terms of time and resources to create and make known a new brand and position yourself on the market (at the beginning you are literally nobody).

Long time to open the shop

2) Open a cannabis shop in Franchising

One choice you can make is to open your company, your shop, relying on a brand that already exists and is known in the market. The name, the brand, the products will be provided to you directly by the "parent" company with which you will continue to have commercial relations dictated by a contract that will bind the two parties.

The cost to open a cannabis shop in Franchising is around € 20,000 / € 25,000

Pros:

- Slightly lower initial investment costs
- Brand already known and placed on the market
- Faster opening times
- Initial training and coaching

Versus:

- Total dependence on the "parent" company in business decisions.

- Affiliate fees.
- Royalty (percentage of turnover to be paid to the franchisor).
- Little flexibility.
- Advertising rights to be recognized to the Franchisor

3) Open a cannabis shop with an intermediate formula

An excellent compromise between opening your own company from scratch and Franchising is the intermediate formula. In this case, an existing brand offers its know- how, logo, graphics, products, initial training and support for starting a business. Unlike franchising, however, it is very flexible. I can therefore also choose only some of the components offered by the "parent" Brand. There is the possibility for example to choose your company name, logo etc. You will then be helped with the opening procedures, any public funding if present, shop setting up, product supply etc.

The cost to open a Cannabis Shop with an intermediate formula varies from € 5,000 to € 20,000

Pros:

- Total flexibility (I can choose whether to be helped totally or only in certain areas).
- Lower initial costs.
- Initial training and coaching.
- No commission on sales.
- Good profit margins.
- Short opening times.

Versus:

- Dependence on the "parent" company in the initial stages.
- Limited decision-making powers regarding company choices.

CHAPTER 13: CANNABIS LIGHT AND MEDICAL CANNABIS.

For cannabis light we mean all those preparations in which the concentrations of THC, or the substance responsible for the psychotropic effect (responsible for the "high" effect), are between 0.2% and 0.6%. It is defined light precisely by virtue of the low concentration of THC when compared to that present in illegally purchased cannabis or cannabis sold in pharmacies and intended for medical use. To convey the idea, the most used product for therapeutic purposes, Bedrocan, has a THC percentage of 22%.

In an interview with Wired, Vincenzo Di Marzo, director of the CNR molecular chemistry institute that has been dealing with the physiological effects of cannabinoids for over 20 years, said:

"The claimed content of Thc is actually very low by comparison, the substances that were smoked in the 60s and 70s contained between 2 and 4% Thc , while the most potent modern herbs, such as skunk, exceed 20% ". And since Thc is the active ingredient responsible for the psychotropic effects of cannabis (and for the damage to neurodevelopment in adolescents and children), it is likely that a "legal joint" has negligible effects.

"However, there is a strong individual variability in the response to the substance, and a certain difference linked to the way the substance is taken, which make it difficult to give a single answer. Much also depends on how the cannabinoid content is measured. In fact, in the plant they are not contained in an active form, but in a non-active, or carboxylated form, which does not produce effects on the nervous system. The transition to the non-carboxylated form occurs with drying and heating, and therefore one should be sure of the percentages of Thc in active form present at the time of consumption, which often involves heating the substance, in order to hypothesize the possible effects on the nervous system ".

The expert concluded his interview by stating that there are not many studies on the pharmacokinetics of Thc , and it is therefore difficult to understand how the repeated consumption of many joints containing very low amounts of Thc would affect the body , compared to the use of smaller doses. of more concentrated substance (typical of currently illegal recreational consumption).

But Marijuana is not all THC, in fact we must not forget about cannabidiol. The situation when we talk about cannabidiol becomes clearer. It is a perfectly legal substance, which has proven antiansiolytic abilities and excellent tolerability. On this Vincenzo Di Marzo declared:

"Studies to date show that it has very few side effects, even at extremely high doses, much higher than those found in cannabis. Suffice it to say that today it is being tested as an antiepileptic for pediatric use. And in some researches, it has been used in doses of 800 milligrams to verify the possible antipsychotic effect, without finding any harmful effects ".

Is there a difference and between medical cannabis and light cannabis?

Medical cannabis and light cannabis differ mainly in the amount of THC and CBD present. This difference means that the therapeutic one can be considered a drug in all respects useful for the control of nausea, vomiting, lack of appetite mainly in patients undergoing chemotherapy and for the control of some forms of chronic pain such as neuropathic pain. Not only that, another indication is that in the treatment of muscle spasticity pains and in cases of fibromyalgia. This effect can only be achieved by consuming cannabis with precise concentrations of THC and CBD.

Furthermore, there is a legal difference between the two types of cannabis. Light hemp can be purchased by any adult, both in physical outlets and in online cannabis stores. Medicinal cannabis can only be bought with a prescription and from pharmacies, and as is well known, the sale is very complex.

The therapeutic effects of hemp are consequently clear and scientifically proven. Light hemp, thanks to the high concentrations of CBD, has or can have positive and relaxing effects that exclude the contraindications and consequently also the therapeutic functions of a high presence of THC, the psychotropic substance that gets you high. Basically, cannabis light thanks to CBD have relaxing and anti-anxiety functions, the therapeutic one is used in a wide range of more or less serious pathologies as a symptomatic treatment.

THE EXTRACTION OF THC RESIN BY THE BUTANE PROCEDURE

Last October, some newspapers began to report this new "trend": the extraction of THC from the inflorescences of light cannabis with butane. As mentioned, the concentration of light cannabis must be less than 0.6%, but according to what these newspapers said, the result would also be 10 times higher (we therefore assume 6%, therefore still much lower than a therapeutic hemp, which is around at 22%). In other articles, however, it was written that the resin produced was about 98% pure by extracting the substance from about 20/30 grams of cannabis light. The article reported that a "doping dose" was formed from 20/30g of light cannabis.

But what is cannabis resin extracted with butane? This resin has a name, BHO or Butane Hash Oil, also known as budder, honey oil, shatter and dab, and is a very powerful cannabis concentrate obtained by butane extraction. This gas is injected under pressure into an elongated, cylindrical container containing marijuana. In this way, the butane is forced to pass through the entire plant material of marijuana, bringing with itself the cannabinoids present in the grass before it is released as a mixture of butane and cannabis. Subsequently, it is left to stand for a few moments to allow the gas to evaporate and, at a later time, it undergoes a purging process, to remove the toxic residues present (such as butane itself) and thus obtain a concentrate of the purest BHO possible.

It is not in our interest to know the extraction procedure, but looking for many more reports and articles, we can say with certainty that this system has been used for many years in the production of BHO with plants that normally have a very high concentration of THC. So what we assume has happened, is that some people have decided to try to use the same procedure on cannabis light to create a finished product, to be considered illegal in the Italian legislature.

However, we believe alarmism is foolish. As stated in various articles and newspapers, for a dose of resin considered illegal it takes about 20/30 grams. On the internet, in one of the online stores, it can be seen that light cannabis costs around 70/80 euros for 10 grams. So to create this narcotic dose, of which the newspapers are so terrified, the cost would be around 150/200 euros. The articles underline the fact that the kit costs 80 euros and the butane cylinders only one euro, but they seem to totally forget the cost of the raw material.

In conclusion, cannabis has carved out a small space in society year after year, moving from taking care of the health of our patients to the recreational use. I am sure that the butane extraction method, which could be useful from the point of view of therapeutic formulations for some of our patients, is not currently a risk or a danger to our society.

In summary. In the United States, medical marijuana growers continue to benefit from the constant aging of the population. Chronic diseases have become more common as the population ages, driving the demand for medical marijuana.

2.6 million people are estimated to use marijuana for medical purposes and this segment of the US population is expected to increase dramatically over the next five years.

More than two-thirds of Americans now live-in jurisdictions that have legalized the medical or recreational use of marijuana.

The industry's revenue is estimated to grow at a rate of 33.5% annually for a turnover of $ 15 billion through 2021.

As of 2016, there are approximately 148,294 companies engaged in the industry in the US, contributing $ 957.6 million in wages and salaries to the nation's economic growth.

As of 2018, 223,123 companies operate in the sector, with approximately 763,189 people employed.

Medical marijuana patients with chronic pain are the largest market segment for the cannabis industry, accounting for 64.6% of the market in 2016, with recreational users accounting for only 14.1% of the market.

The remaining market share is shared by consumers who purchase products for the treatment and management of other pains.

According to data released by Forbes, in 2017 the trade in legal marijuana around the world grew by 37% and was worth $ 9.5 billion.

With sales of approximately $ 8.5 billion, the United States accounts for 90% of the medical cannabis market.

With a turnover of around €0.6 billion Canada's market shares in 2017 was 6%. The rest of the world holds the remaining 4% of the market.

CHAPTER 14: WHAT TO SELL IN A GROW SHOP

Opening a grow shop is one of the business opportunities that at the moment seems to involve and interest various people throughout Italy. In fact, these shops dedicated to the sale of legal cannabis, its derivatives, marijuana-based foods and products and oils for physical well-being and beauty always deriving from cannabis.

But are grow shops legal? More and more people are wondering if the sale of light cannabis is really legal and if opening one of these shops does not lead to problems with the police. This activity in Italy is legal, or rather there is no law prohibiting the sale of cannabis inflorescences with a THC content lower than that considered illegal by law.

The limit THC content is 0.6%, so in these shops you can sell all products that derive from hemp, as long as their content of this cannabinoid is below the limit imposed by law.

HOW TO OPEN A GROW SHOP: PROCEDURE AND LEGAL PRECAUTIONS

Being a relatively recent activity, opening a grow shop is considered a good form of investment, but before opening a shop of this kind it is necessary to take into consideration some precautions that allow you to start a totally legal business and that does not risk closure. In fact, unlike other shops dedicated to the trade of traditional goods, grow shops are considered to be at risk of illegal activities, for this reason they are constantly monitored by the police who control the type of goods sold.

Given this particular attention of the police forces, to open a grow shop in addition to having to follow the classic bureaucratic process required for the opening of a commercial activity (Registration with the Chamber of Commerce, opening of Inps and Inail positions, municipal authorization permits etc ...) you must also pay attention to the products you buy.

All products should only be purchased from vendors who can certify that all hemp products do not contain a THC value greater than 0.6%. Furthermore, it is always recommended to keep all invoices, receipts and documents certifying that the cannabis you are selling is light and that the product has been purchased regularly.

As we have mentioned, grow shops can sell all light cannabis products. These stores are primarily supposed to market light cannabis growing and gardening equipment. In fact, you can sell seeds, the right land, lamps to encourage growth, irrigation systems, etc.

In addition to gardening products, you can also sell inflorescences, and specialize for example in the sale of items for smokers, choosing to also market lighters, bongs, hookahs or vaporizers, but also papers and everything you need to smoke.

In addition to these products, you can also choose to sell food products such as: hemp flour, beer and marijuana drinks, cannabis jam, supplements, etc. For the sale of these products, however, it is necessary to ask for permits for the opening of a commercial activity, also the permission to sell and supply drinks and food.

Finally, many of these stores also offer a wide range of beneficial products made with marijuana, in fact it is possible to sell oils, creams, ointments, make-up and cosmetics.

What Is A Grow Shop?

A grow shop is a retail store specializing in the sale of equipment and supplies for growing plants especially indoors.

Although grow shops are known as specialized shops for growing cannabis, in reality the products marketed are suitable for all types of crops such as horticulture.

The grow shop has an extensive catalog ranging from various substrate soils, to fertilizers, lamps, hydroponic systems, etc.

In addition to all the growing material, grow shops often offer other products such as hemp food, cosmetics and the now famous cannabis light.

The first grow shops were started in the USA during the 1950s during the first marijuana boom, a phenomenon that arrived about 20 years late in Europe, especially in countries more tolerant of DIY cannabis cultivation such as Spain and Holland.

Grow shops are an example of contradiction in a country like Italy where certain activities such as the cultivation of cannabis is prohibited in theory, but in parallel has a thriving sector such as grow shops.

Finally, after decades of contradictions, the European law 242 of December 2016 has brought some certainties about the cultivation of cannabis.

Despite continuing doubts and legislative interpretations, the first clear stakes have been defined and that is, that in Italy the cultivation of cannabis is allowed as long as the plant derives from a certified seed with a special tag that certifies the origin of the seed that was originally selected, to contain a percentage lower than 0.6% of THC, the psychoactive substance of cannabis present in the inflorescence.

Despite decades of scientific literature, we have now shown that THC is a substance that is not only harmless, but even beneficial for the treatment of many diseases, in Italy there is still an obscurantist lobby that fights against complete legalization.

We must understand this timeless lobby, it is now an active part in the defense of certain clear and obvious interests such as the multinationals of pharmaceuticals and plastics that fear the spread of a plant that is not only harmless, but capable of undermining the monopoly of certain characters.

In fact, hemp produces medicines, fabrics, building materials, bio fuels, seed oil and much more.

Despite the lobbying that attacks hemp, the law is now on the side of producers and therefore the road to the future has been traced as Canada, California, Uruguay, Holland and Spain have already shown.

Pending a complete legalization, today the legal situation of the grow shops is absolutely calm as long as you follow the law and market products normally on the market.

If there are no problems with regards to the equipment, if the trader decides to sell inflorescences of light cannabis, he must pay attention to the producer and always ask for the analyses that certify the level of THC contained.

CHAPTER 15: OPENING A DISPENSARY IN ILLINOIS COST

What are the costs of opening a cannabis business in Illinois?

Opening a cannabis dispensary in Illinois costs $ 500,000 to $ 1,000,000.

Opening a Cannabis Dispensary in Illinois will be expensive due to the costs of security, capital requirements, licensing, consulting, and legal costs, which continue in your company's operations.

Get ready and build a great team and a business plan and get the right consultants and resources for your success.

The experts we spoke to believe that the costs to open your cannabis business in Illinois will range from $ 400,000 to $ 1,000,000 for a dispensary and from $ 1.5 million to $ 3.0 million for artisanal grow shops, depending on your location and size of buildings.

Each state is a little different, but if you want to open a dispensary or a grow shop in Illinois, the regulations and limited number of licenses add to the cost more than on the West Coast.

What are the costs of opening a dispensary?

Here is a quick rundown of the startup costs for opening a cannabis dispensary or craft growing in Illinois:

- Statutory commissions
- Costs of compiling the application
- Legal fees
- Cannabis Operations Advisor Fees
- Fees for accountants and other professionals
- Insurance premiums
- Community outreach costs
- Properly capitalized requirements
- Construction of buildings and fixed rental costs
- Employees
- Costs of flowers and inventory
- Renewal license fees
- Taxes (IRC 280E)
- Marketing
- Professional commissions in progress
- Licensing fees for your cannabis dispensary or Craft Grow

These are the simplest costs: the taxes you pay to the state of Illinois. They are provided for by statute and have a number. Simple to plug into your budget, but that's just the tip-to-toe cost of your cannabis companies to open their dispensary or grow artisanally.

For dispensaries:

- Non-refundable application fee of $ 5,000.
- $ 60,000 registration fee (renewable for the same amount every two years.)

For Craft Grows:

- Non-refundable application fee of $ 5,000.
- $ 40,000 application fee (becomes renewable fee)

Location of your cannabis dispensary or craft cultivation

Real estate is all about location, so where you open your cannabis business is important. Rent, because cannabis businesses cannot finance a mortgage for them

Your dispensary square footage will impact your double taxation under IRC 280E and also your rental costs. Although growers are not impressed with IRC 280E, they must maintain buildings within closed loop system buildings if they are to maintain the highest quality product.

You have to plan and imagine your cannabis business very precisely, with the help of talented designers and architects, to determine not only your startup needs, but also your daily operating costs.

Expect a market rent premium and possible zoning problems. Fortunately, dispensaries in Illinois have six months from the granting of their conditional use dispensing license to provide the state with its address.

Also, the security issues regarding the location of your property should be explored and discussed in your question because security is an important point under your score. The same goes for the configurations and security features needed to be integrated into your craft dispensing or growing business, which isn't as stringent in West Coast states. The costs of furniture, fixtures and equipment (FF&E) in Illinois are higher due to the precise level of security built into the law to prevent the diversion of cannabis from the supply chain or the robberies of adult-only cannabis-using money.

Complete the application for an Illinois Dispensary or Craft Grow

The consultants will help you put together your cannabis license application, business plan, financial plans, security plans, social equity plans, and numerous other things. The completed question will resemble what was known as a "rubric" in the 20th century. The phrase means that a high-scoring application's stack of papers will be large, perhaps hundreds of pages.

The reason for the length of the application has to do with the promises your cannabis business is making to the State of Illinois (and your state if you are elsewhere) about its application. Upon issuing a license to grow or distribute cannabis in your business, all the terms and conditions and promises regarding your cannabis business that you have made in the application actually become requirements to run your business!

Your application requires employee training policies, public awareness plans, security design and protocols, sophisticated business operations, property and financial contracts, and important record keeping systems and procedures employed in growing or selling the adult who they use cannabis. No other company has so many pre- plans to be licensed to open its doors.

If you've ever heard an entrepreneur complain about overly burdensome regulations, ask if they're in the cannabis industry.

The application process can cost tens of thousands of dollars and will be described in more detail below. The important thing your business can do when taking the risk of applying for a license is at least to purchase a good application. Illinois has very few places open for the first wave of the industry. Maybe you will do the first wave, or the second, or the third.

If Illinois becomes like Colorado, the number of dispensary and craft production licenses will have to triple about the current legal maximums, which means people like you will need to continue lobbying the state to update and amend the law to more players.

CANNABIS BUSINESS (TEAM) PLAN

When drafting your business plan, use this team mindset when combining: your culture, your key legal, tax, security and operational advisors, your investors and, of course, your clients.

Illinois adds a new wrinkle to the traditional cannabis business plans of other adult consumption states: social equity. You can use social equity goals to open up the cannabis industry to those who have been most influenced by drug laws over the past 80 years. Perhaps your cannabis company will come up with a plan to hire 10 full-time candidates for social equity so that your company can be proudly recognized for helping meet the state's goals in its new adult use law.

Of course, the business plan should have traditional revenue and expense projections and a financial planner or CPA with previous retail experience, and hopefully cannabis, the experience will bring your company's most reliable data. Cannabis business plans, unlike simple business plans, often have to address aspects of the business resulting from regulatory compliance. For example, you will have compliance costs to ensure that your operations comply with new and evolving laws in its operations and how they can be detailed as those managed by software or human resources.

SAFETY PLAN FOR THE DISTRIBUTION OF CANNABIS OR ARTISANAL CULTIVATION

Security doesn't just mean having a burly guy with a gun. Security blends best practices in technology, structural design, and law enforcement surveillance to implement a system that, if something goes wrong, who did it, when it was done, and what exactly happened is all captured in high definition, printed and provided to law enforcement authorities.

Security is also built into your property in its layout, customer experience stream, doors, cameras, strobes, building materials, and even employee training policies and procedures. The security plan aspect of your application counts for many points. Cannabis businesses cost a lot to open, but the initial cost is to fill out the right safety plan so that it meets your state's approval and high score.

Record-keeping plan to prevent the diversion of cannabis or money

Many companies have proprietary software that was invented before Illinois even became a medical cannabis state. These are the ancillary activities that arise when cannabis becomes a legal activity. The software you will use to track product supply and sales will depend on the consultant you choose. You don't want your Point of Sale (POS) system to be a real, well, POS.

If your business plan includes developing such technologies in its five-year plans to create additional revenue streams by selling licenses for what it creates, then you should call me unless you are thinking of doing it in C #. Then you can hire someone else or provide a detailed reason for your choice of that language.

Employee training plans and policies should also have best practices in place that provide accurate cannabis registration. These procedures must be followed and include training with whatever software your business has decided to use to track their inventory and sales. Familiarity with your systems is key to preventing cannabis from being hijacked down the supply chain or going bad by taking up shelf space with products that should have cleared faster.

FINANCIAL ABILITY TO DESIGN, BUILD AND MANAGE CANNABIS BUSINESSES

The application to obtain your license to grow or dispense cannabis includes many projects and plans for your facility and perhaps the packaging and labeling of the product. Designers are very important to the image and look they can convey for your new cannabis brand. So having them draw up plans for your property or product packaging won't be cheap. But if your application is successful, it gets even more expensive because projects now have to be built and used.

With or without access to loans and grants available to "qualified social equity applicants", all licensed cannabis companies must prove their financial capacity to carry out their projects and make them a reality. This cost is specific and unique to your particular brand, its design and the location of the properties.

Regardless of whether your cannabis business is highly cost-conscious or well-funded, you need to be able to demonstrate that you have the money to carry out your projects and application specifications, including payroll financing for your operations.

Employee Handbook and Educational Policies Required by Illinois Cannabis Law

Many companies build their employment practices and manuals as they grow over time, but cannabis companies need to have them in place before opening their doors.

Training your cannabis employees is another step in setting your brand for the customer experience, but it also draws on your safety policies by teaching practices for observing the person's body language and actions to remember certain details in case something goes wrong.

Further employee education and training can guide policies to reduce and recognize theft and protect employees and customers in the event of a robbery.

Of course, budtenders should have knowledge of the flower and its extracts, terpenoid profiles and strains so that they can advise clients on what kind of experience they intend to gain from cannabis.

Employee training policies can help you make your customers happy, state regulators happy, and your business safe.

Community Commitment / Social Equity Plan to Achieve the Goals of the Illinois Cannabis Law

While not many points are specifically enumerated for community outreach, and in some cases the points are simply bonuses in the event of a tie, which means you should still do it. If you tied and didn't include it, but the other candidate did, bad luck!

What does your cannabis company do to give back? There are many things you can do to educate people, or help those harmed by the damage caused by the war on drugs, or another woman, minority, veteran or disabled group.

Provide funding for this engagement plan in your business operations budget, as it should be an ongoing expense that your business continues to make to enrich the community it serves.

COSTS FOR CANNABIS EMPLOYEES

Dispensary managers must keep the business running smoothly in a compliant manner. They deal with employees, customers, vendors, state regulators, business owners, perhaps even investors. They are in demand due to the scarcity of the industry, but consultants estimate that for a dispensary, annual staff costs can reach the range of a quarter of a million dollars.

There are both upfront costs and ongoing costs. You need a lawyer, an accountant, an operations consultant and you need to be properly insured. Annual budgets for these range in the tens of thousands of dollars.

COSTS TO PROMOTE YOUR CANNABIS BUSINESS

Not just SEO, social media outreach, design and YouTube, you can sponsor community outreach events to build your brand. Our favorite is sponsoring expungement seminars and job fairs in partnership with local lawyer associations, politicians and cannabis companies. Remember to include these things into your plans and set yourself apart from the competition.

Summary of the costs of entering the legal cannabis market in Illinois

So now you understand why we said it would average around $ 500,000 to open a cannabis dispensary in Illinois. We didn't actually get into all the costs of the growing equipment that can mount due to the various HVAC and machinery, and the safety, construction requirements of a craft grow. That average will likely be around $ 2,000,000, but it depends on the characteristics the grow wants to offer.

CHAPTER 16: HOW TO OBTAIN A COMMERCIAL LICENSE FOR CANNABIS IN NEW JERSEY

The people of New Jersey voted and a new cannabis legalization law passed! - Get ready to receive your licensed cannabis business to start operating in New Jersey.

New Jersey immediately got new legislation to codify people's votes. Question 1 was approved with 66.91% of the votes. The cannabis market is opening up in the state, it is your opportunity to start preparing your license application to open your cannabis business.

The cannabis industry is changing a lot when it comes to its regulations, New Jersey is no exception. The regulations are still being drafted and there are many important details to be determined, so we can expect many updates on legalization in New Jersey in the coming months.

CONSTITUTIONAL AMENDMENT FOR THE LEGALIZATION OF MARIJUANA

Do you approve of the Constitution amendment to legalize a controlled form of marijuana called "cannabis"?

Only adults 21 years of age or older could use cannabis. The state commission created to oversee the state medical cannabis program would also oversee the new cannabis market for personal use.

Cannabis products would be subject to state sales tax. If authorized by the legislature, a municipality can pass a local ordinance to charge a local tax on cannabis products.

INTERPRETIVE STATEMENT

This amendment would legalize a controlled form of marijuana called "cannabis". Only people 21 years of age or older could legally use cannabis products.

The Cannabis Regulatory Commission would oversee the new adult cannabis market. This commission was created in 2019 to oversee the state's medical cannabis program. The scope of the new Commission authority would be detailed in the laws enacted by the legislature.

All retail sales of cannabis products in the new adult cannabis market would be subject to state sales tax. If authorized by the legislature, a municipality can pass a local ordinance to charge a local tax on cannabis products.

CHAPTER 17: IDEAS FOR WORKING WITH LEGAL CANNABIS

If you are passionate about cannabis, this is probably one of the most exciting times you can live in. The legal marijuana industry is growing like wildfire, creating new businesses and numerous job opportunities.

So, if you've always dreamed of working with marijuana (instead of just smoking it) now is the time to step forward. Here are some business ideas for the cannabis industry to help you get your creativity flowing and kickstart your life as a cannabis entrepreneur.

1. DESIGN OF SALES POINTS

Legalization is showing us that the term " stoner " should be banned and marijuana accessible to all. More and more people, from the parents of footballers to the most skilled professionals, are showing greater openness to cannabis. As a result, people expect a lot more from cannabis shops.

That's why we're starting to see a complete revamp of dispensaries, coffeeshops, and other cannabis retailers. Dispensaries in the US and coffeeshops in the Netherlands are decorating their interiors with increasingly modern styles and furnishings to attract a new type of cannabis customer.

Stores that sell cannabis are changing their strategies to present themselves to the public through novel design. This has created a growing demand for talented designers with professional qualifications and a broad understanding of this particular industry, but also for international designers who are passionate about cannabis and eager to work in this environment.

2. COSMETICS

If you've been living in a cave for the past couple of years, here's some outdated news that might interest you: Cannabis cosmetics are hugely successful.

The benefits of cannabis cosmetics and the compounds they contain are amply demonstrated by a solid research base. Furthermore, the therapeutic properties of cannabinoids such as THC and CBD (pain relievers, anti-inflammatory, etc.) are supported by a lot of research and our body can benefit from them topically in the form of balms, sprays, lotions and more.

These important developments have given birth to a new and gigantic market for medicinal and beauty products. In fact, there are many brands specialized in cannabis-based beauty products on the market. Lord Jones, Khus Khus and Vertly are only a small part of those now established in this niche market.

The Body Shop brand has also caught on in the industry with its new line of cannabis creams and balms, not to mention actress Whoopi Goldberg who launched her medical marijuana products, including bubble baths, body balms and more.

As the cannabis industry grows and becomes more and more competitive, companies do their best to make their business more effective and outperform the competition.

And just as companies in other sectors rely on branding experts, designers, copywriters and advertisers, cannabis companies target the same professionals. From dispensaries to seedbanks, and everything in between, companies are constantly looking for tailor-made services to develop attractive brands and drive sales of their products / services.

This is very encouraging news for marketers looking to expand into a new industry. If you fit into this professional profile, working as a freelancer or starting your own agency could be a very promising business idea.

3. CONSULTING

There are, of course, endless regulations drawn up to legally produce, manage and sell cannabis. Not to mention the regulations for its marketing, for the places where it is consumed and much more. If you live in the United States, these regulations can drastically change from one state to another.

Above these legal gray areas, the production and sale of cannabis-related products remains a challenge in itself. Cultivating the plant alone is quite challenging, especially for those who are unfamiliar with the plant but still want to compete on the commercial playground.

This situation is worrying young entrepreneurs looking to enter the marijuana market. Fortunately, in these cases a consultant may be the most sought-after professional figure. There is an increasing need for consultants with expertise in the cannabis sector who are able to help new businesses overcome market obstacles.

If you are an experienced grower, for example, you could advise emerging producers on the deep and growing developments in professional cannabis cultivation. If you're a cannabis lawyer, you have what it takes to help companies navigate the treacherous sea of legal minutiae.

4. TECHNOLOGY

The legal cannabis industry is still quite recent. While the technology of many other sectors has evolved for centuries, technological solutions for the cannabis industry have only been openly developed in recent years.

Of course, some have already begun to adopt technology solutions for businesses and, for example, have created comprehensive technology packages specifically designed to help dispensaries and other cannabis businesses automate and optimize their businesses, using technology for e- commerce, CMS and more.

Other examples of how companies are renovating the cannabis industry include agencies developing software for marijuana outlets.

And while the cannabis industry is becoming increasingly competitive, there are still many ways the technology could help track the management and sale of this plant more quickly. If you are tech savvy, get your ideas together and step forward.

5. CANNABIS EVENT ORGANIZERS

We have written about the extension of cannabis communities on repeated occasions and that is why we see so much excitement among the agencies that organize cannabis events.

Cannabis users are constantly looking for fun gatherings where they can share their love of weed and do different activities, such as painting under the effects of marijuana or cycling tours in favor of the legalization of this plant.

But there are still tons of other job opportunities for creative event organizers where they can come up with the best tactics for combining cannabis with other exciting activities. So if you have a penchant for organizing large events, this might be your chance.

6. EDIBLES AND CANNABIS-BASED COOKING

If there's one thing we all agree on, it's that cannabis and food are like peaches and cream. If you think like us and are passionate about finding new and intriguing ways to combine cannabis and food, this professional profile could be for you.

Like cosmetics and concentrates (which we'll discuss in the next section of this list), the cannabis market for edibles and other food products is huge. In addition to producers of cannabis-based foods, even the most creative entrepreneurs are starting to give cannabis cooking classes, seminars on how to combine the various foods and more.

This is an extremely exciting way to enter the legal cannabis market, without necessarily becoming a grower or a retailer of buds.

7. CONCENTRATES AND EXTRACTS OF CANNABIS

Another huge chunk of the cannabis market revolves around extracts. " Dabbing " is certainly one of the most popular trends in the industry, another quite creative alternative to get into this business.

The concentrate market offers the most diverse job opportunities. Of course, you could create your own brand of extracts. However, it is also possible to specialize in the production of machinery and equipment for extraction, or to advise those who would like to enter the market. There are numerous business ventures involving the creation, management and sale of concentrates.

8. ART AND CANNABIS RELATED ITEMS

The cannabis industry has supported the rise of extraordinary artists, including Tony Greenhand, the artistic joint rolling professional, and numerous other glass artists who specialize in producing carefully crafted items sold at exorbitant prices around the world.

Cannabis has also made its way into high fashion and among the giants of "fast fashion", with some clothes that can reach unprecedented figures. Currently, the art world is experiencing a major resurgence in marijuana-inspired projects across various disciplines. If you are a creative person interested in combining your passion for art and cannabis, this is yet another field of research to consider to be successful in the "cane business".

9. OPEN A BED & BREAKFAST FOR CANNABIS LOVERS

In countries where marijuana regulations have changed in recent years, more and more cannabis tourists are looking for comfortable accommodations to spend their holidays. If you live in one of these places, you may want to set up a facility to accommodate cannabis smokers.

Decorate the rooms according to what you think a cannabis lover might appreciate and always offer something special. You could possibly sell local handicrafts.

So, if you have a passion for cannabis and have always wanted to be part of this industry, now is the time to step up. The market is booming and if you think you have the necessary requirements, please jump at the opportunity.

CHAPTER 18: HOW TO OBTAIN A MEDICAL MARIJUANA CARD IN THE UNITED STATES

As of 2019, 33 US states have legalized some form of medical marijuana. Each state has a different legal framework governing medical marijuana. Therefore, it is important to be aware of all local marijuana rules, laws and requirements before you can obtain a card and purchase medical marijuana.

Despite the fact that it remains federally illegal, medical marijuana is now legal in 33 US states, and Washington DC Each state has developed its own legal framework for governing the medical marijuana system. While there are similarities between the legal frameworks applied in each state, there are also important differences. It is incredibly important to make sure you understand your state's rules and regulations.

Having a medical marijuana card exempts you from most statewide marijuana possession and consumption laws. However, the qualification conditions and the process for obtaining a card differ from state to state. If your state does not recognize your specific illness, buying outside of the state is not an option.

The following states have legalized medical marijuana:

Legal Medical Cannabis

Alaska (1) - Arizona (2) - Arkansas (3) - California (4) - Colorado (5) - Connecticut (6) - Delaware (7) - Florida (8) - Hawaii (9) - Illinois (10) - Louisiana (11) - Maine (12) - Maryland (13) - Massachusetts (14) - Michigan (15) - Minnesota (16) - Missouri (17) - Montana (18) - Nevada (19) - New Hampshire (20) - New Jersey (21) - New Mexico (22) - New York (23) - North Dakota (24) - Ohio (25) - Oklahoma (26) - Oregon (27) - Pennsylvania (28) - Rhode Island (29) - Utah (30) - Vermont (31) - Washington (32) - West Virginia (33) - Washington DC (34).

WHAT DO YOU NEED TO GET A MEDICAL MARIJUANA CARD?

The answer to this question will largely depend on the state you live in. However, there are some things that will be required of you in every state. Regardless of the state you are in, you will be required to: know the requirements, prepare the correct documentation and obtain a legal prescription.

LOOK FOR THE REGULATIONS AND RESTRICTIONS OF YOUR STATE

Make sure you have a thorough understanding of your state's medical marijuana regulations, requirements, and restrictions. Having this information in advance can help you avoid potential obstacles or surprises in the future. It will also allow you to carry out the application process in a faster and more peaceful way.

To get a medical marijuana card, you must have a qualified medical condition. The conditions required for a medical card can vary extremely from state to state. Your state's health services office will most likely be able to provide you with an up-to-date list of accepted conditions.

COLLECT THE REQUIRED DOCUMENTATION

You will need to provide adequate medical and legal documentation. During the process, any previous medical records documenting your illness may be helpful or even necessary. Your physician or a representative of your state's health department may be able to tell you exactly what documents will be needed in your jurisdiction.

You will also need proper legal identification, such as a driver's license or passport. Additionally, you will need to provide proof of residency.

GET A PRESCRIPTION FROM YOUR DOCTOR

You need to get approval from a registered doctor, which may not always be an easy thing to do, as many doctors are not yet willing to prescribe medical marijuana. In these situations, you may be able to find a clinic or doctor who specializes in medical marijuana prescriptions. Having a medical document to support a claim for a disease can be helpful in obtaining a prescription.

In most states, medical marijuana cards are only valid for a specific period of time. Remember the expiration date of your card and take some time to look for your state's renewal process. Doing this in advance can prevent you from finding yourself without a valid card for any length of time.

WHAT MEDICAL CONDITIONS QUALIFY YOU FOR MEDICAL MARIJUANA?

The qualifying medical conditions required to obtain a medical marijuana card differ from state to state. Here are some of the most common diseases that medical marijuana is prescribed for in the United States:

ANXIETY, ANOREXIA AND DIETARY PROBLEMS, ARTHRITIS, AIDS / HIV, CHRONIC PAIN, CANCER,

EPILEPSY AND CONVULSIVE DISORDERS, GLAUCOMA, MULTIPLE SCLEROSIS, NAUSEA, NEURODEGENERATIVE DISEASES, POST-TRAUMATIC STRESS.

HOW CAN YOU GET THE MEDICAL MARIJUANA CARD ONLINE?

In some states, such as California and Florida, you may be able to get a medical marijuana card online. This process will save you time by connecting directly to a doctor who specializes in medical marijuana. In addition, it will allow you to get a card from the comfort of your home. Some online clinics may even give you an immediate recommendation, allowing you to purchase legal marijuana on the same day. If you're looking to get the procedure done as quickly and conveniently as possible, an online clinic may be your best choice.

In most cases, the process is very quick and straightforward. After providing your identification, medical information and proof of residency, you will be subjected to a personal online assessment. These assessments typically last from 5 to 15 minutes and involve a series of questions. The main purpose of these assessments is to clearly establish your medical situation and why marijuana could improve it.

Once your request has been accepted, you can expect to receive your card in the mail within a few days. However, in some states you will be able to legally purchase medical marijuana immediately after receiving an email confirmation. Often this means being able to purchase marijuana on the same day as the valuation. Talk to your doctor and local dispensaries to find out what their exact policy is regarding email recommendations.

CAN YOU TRAVEL WITH MEDICAL CANNABIS?

CAN TOURISTS QUALIFY FOR A MEDICAL MARIJUANA CARD?

No. The United States requires proof of residency when licensing medical marijuana. Hence, out-of-state tourists will not be able to successfully obtain medical marijuana licenses.

However, in some states, tourists from other states who have valid medical marijuana cards and identification can purchase marijuana legally. States like California, Arizona, and Washington sell recreational or medical marijuana to all tourists of legal age. However, traveling from state to state with legally purchased marijuana is not yet recommended.

In September 2018, the Arizona Appeals Court ruled that out-of-state medical marijuana licenses would be recognized within its state. If you're traveling to a state that has recreational marijuana, your medical state doesn't matter. However, if you intend to purchase medical marijuana, check local laws and regulations to make sure your medical license is accepted in the state you are visiting.

CHAPTER 19: DO YOU WANT TO GROW HEMP LEGALLY? HERE ARE SOME TIPS AND INDICATIONS

Nowadays, light hemp is undoubtedly one of the trendiest crops in Italy, and it is enough to take a look at the latest cannabis cultivation statistics to realize how thriving the market is.

To demonstrate this, it is also useful to share some reflections with the main associations that bring together small farmers and large farms: they will confirm that there are more and more operators who declare themselves extremely interested in participating in this sector, and that they are always more people who have decided to discover how to grow cannabis in order to benefit from the many beneficial properties that this plant substance is able to give us.

In fact, despite the countless criticisms that come from some of the media and public opinion, not everyone knows that light hemp can bring many advantages: we remember that this plant has pain-relieving, anti-nausea, anti-inflammatory properties and, moreover, can be a great help against migraines.

Growing cannabis, so many benefits from growing weed!

According to some scientific studies, moreover, it would seem that the results of cannabis cultivation can inhibit tumor growth since it causes apoptosis, or the death of malignant cells (but, beware, further studies are needed to be able to consciously ascertain this and, therefore, we cannot do more than advise you to talk to your doctor for the latest updates on this topic!).

Precisely for these reasons there are so many people who have discovered how to grow cannabis legally and have chosen to enter this sector in a lawful way, obtaining their evident satisfaction.

It is by virtue of the above that hemp crops are growing more and more all over the world: in the United States there has been a significant increase in crops, constant in recent years, but at the same time - driven by more favorable legislation - also in Italy, companies that know better and better how cannabis is grown and how to make use of these experiences.

Hemp cultivation, a simple and affordable practice for (almost) everyone

On the other hand, light hemp is a very simple plant to grow, since it grows easily and produces inflorescences for a good part of the year. Furthermore, this plant does not need particular climatic conditions to grow luxuriantly, and for this reason it can be grown in any suitably equipped space, even indoors.

As far as the legal aspects are concerned, nowadays installing a legitimate hemp cultivation is very simple, considering that it is sufficient to go through a rather lean authorization process to be able to obtain the licenses that allow you to start a cannabis cultivation business without running into any problems of a legal nature, and therefore being able to conduct an agricultural entrepreneurial initiative that has the same characteristics as any business linked to the "land".

Of course, before embarking on this area it is necessary to be aware of all the regulations in force, in order not to risk making mistakes and having to deal with drastic "corrections".

To grow hemp legally it is therefore necessary to take into account simple but fundamental precautions, which we will summarize below, inviting all those who are interested to get very well informed, in advance, to know how to grow light hemp legally or to understand how to produce it at home.

Cannabis cultivation: how to grow cannabis seeds in Italy without risk

The first thing to do, if you want to find out how to grow cannabis at home, is to find out about the laws in force in Italy in relation to hemp plants.

In this context, it should be remembered that nowadays it is no longer necessary to have the authorization for the cultivation of cannabis legally by the police and that, therefore, you can therefore begin to produce it at home without being afraid of legal repercussions.

Therefore, you no longer need to hide: light hemp can also be grown in the home, if all the other requirements set by current legislation are respected. Good news for those who are trying these days to evaluate whether or not this can be a profitable path for their professional interests.

Furthermore, there are numerous varieties available that are sold in Italy and that come from certified seeds, thus allowing the satisfaction of any declination - even the most specific - of one's cannabis cultivation business.

The origin of the seeds

We recall in this regard that everyone can start the cultivation of cannabis as long as the latter is characterized by seeds certified by the European Union.

If, on the other hand, the seeds are not present on the "approved" list, then it will not be possible to cultivate them fully legally, therefore making it necessary to proceed with the selection of another variety (considering the vast range available today, we are sure that you will have no problems in identifying the one for you!).

To choose a light hemp variety, however, you must also understand what result you intend to obtain, since they are all different in terms of cultivation characteristics. Usually, the most used variety in recent times is the dioecious, which is able to develop both male and female varieties, but on different plants (therefore both characters will not be produced on the same plant).

If you want to produce the inflorescences you will need to proceed with a job called unmasking, which basically consists in eliminating the males from the field, since it is the female plants that produce the largest and best inflorescences, if these are not pollinated by their male colleagues.

The above is an extremely important process, since preventing the male from pollinating the female allows the female plants to raise their quality to a much more appreciated and sought-after stage.

If, on the other hand, a person wants to produce hemp from seed, he can prefer both dioecious and monoecious varieties: the latter are used to reproduce the seed of a certain genetics while the former are usually used to have a seed to be used in the cosmetic field or food.

What are the regulations that allow you to grow hemp legally?

Having clarified the above, let's try to take another step forward in deepening cannabis cultivation and ask ourselves what are the regulations that today allow us to grow hemp legally.

We therefore specify, as you should have well understood by reading the previous lines, that to grow hemp legally at your home it is advisable to know the regulations in force on the subject and the latest updates on the subject. Fortunately, however, today the Italian legal discipline is much more generous than in the past, and it is certainly more open to this world than it was in the past.

In addition to doing what we have already mentioned, which is to grow the seeds on the list approved by the European Union, you will also need to make sure that the seeds do not contain THC higher than 0.2%.

Remember that if your seeds do not contain more than 0.2% THC you will not need any authorization to grow cannabis. You must also keep in mind to always keep the tags of the seeds you buy (along with the invoices) for at least twelve months.

What if you go over the 0.2% THC limit?

If, on the other hand, the plants that will be obtained from cultivation contain a THC value lower than or equal to 0.6%, the farmer will still have no legal repercussions, but will have to proceed towards a more specific authorization process.

In particular, it is also possible that the authorities want to carry out tests to see if the THC value is actually within the norm. In this case, however, they will have to leave a sample to the grower so that they can perform possible counter-checks, for their own protection.

We also note that according to the law in force, and according to subsequent clarifications by the Ministry of

Agricultural Policies, it is possible to grow light hemp without the need for authorization but cultivation by cuttings is prohibited: this term indicates a part of a plant which is introduced into the soil and which can create another individual plant.

Those who want to produce inflorescences can decide between different varieties. The most used are Carmagnola, Eletta Campana, Finola, Kompolti and Tisza. You have to keep in mind, however, that Finola is used more for late sowing since it has an extremely short cycle and therefore allows you to have a harvest three months after planting.

Those who want to grow light hemp outdoors, on the other hand, can use other varieties that have a greater development such as Kompolti which can reach up to seven meters in height and can be grown in 130 days depending on the area in which the cultivation takes place. If, on the other hand, you want to produce a seed that can be used for food or cosmetic use, you can use varieties such as Fedora, Uzo 31 or Felina.

Where to get the seeds to grow light hemp legally

In the last few lines, we have focused on the fact that in order to grow light hemp in a legal way it is necessary to buy seeds certified by the Ministry of Agricultural Policies and by the European Union.

Today, the purchase can take place in two ways: in the shop or at agricultural seed dealers. The latter, in fact, have most of the hemp varieties or at least the most used ones.

Another very simple way to buy seeds is to use the internet: online there are many retailers of light hemp seeds that also come from abroad (many varieties in fact originate both in Eastern Europe and in France) and that they will open the door to a range of alternatives that you probably never suspected could exist!

However, it is good to remember that before making the online purchase it is advisable to carefully check that the seeds are actually legal in Italy. Furthermore, we must not forget that it is not possible to use the cuttings except for ornamental purposes. Therefore, if you want a cutting to create a hemp plant to display in your home as a decorative object, you will have no problem, but if you need the cuttings for the production of hemp you will have to abandon the idea and use seeds or sprouts instead.

Choosing the right terrain

The right soil is also an element that should not be underestimated when you want to grow this type of plant. It is usually advisable to choose a medium-textured one, which is therefore composed of sand, clay and silt divided into equal parts. Of course, the soil must also be well prepared and worked in such a way as to be able to adequately accommodate the cultivation of hemp. The latter also does not need a lot of water; therefore, it is not mandatory to irrigate. However, it is always good to keep in mind that climatic conditions can change and therefore a drip irrigation system could be the ideal solution. For fertilization, on the other hand, it is possible to use manure or a phosphorus-based fertiliser that can significantly promote flowering.

Also remember that more and more people are discovering the possibility of growing cannabis thanks to coconut fiber, as we documented in our recent study, or growing cannabis in aeroponics, without soil.

What you need to know for growing light hemp

Finally, it must be remembered that light flowering hemp must be harvested manually and in a delicate way, since it is necessary to preserve its quality and value. If you use machinery, in fact, you could risk ruining the inflorescence! Seed hemp, on the other hand, can be harvested either manually or by means of machines that are made specifically for the cultivation of hemp.

Furthermore, in both cases it is advisable to create dryers, since the seeds need to be dried after harvesting. You must remember that to carry out this operation you will need a professional dryer as this is one of the most important processes that will help you to obtain quality light hemp.

To grow light hemp legally at home, you can use different methods. One of the simplest to put into practice concerns the use of LED lamps and grow boxes. The latter are basically greenhouses that have particular ventilation systems and that can also be kept safely at home.

The use of LED lamps, on the other hand, can also bring various benefits to those who grow light hemp. First of all, this system involves a lower expenditure of electricity which therefore translates into a lower cost on the bill. In addition to this, LED lamps allow for a higher quality of light: this means that the harvest will also be significantly better. Finally, with Led lamps it is also possible to cultivate in all months of the year without the need for particular climatic conditions. No less important is the reduced risk of pest attacks that could ruin the cultivation of light hemp.

Conclusions

In short, if you want to grow hemp at home, and you want to do it legally, today you have many possibilities at your disposal.

The regulatory interventions that have occurred over the last few years have increasingly favored the possibility of independently starting the cultivation of legal cannabis, provided - of course - you respect the regulatory requirements in force, which in any case are not excessively stringent and they will therefore allow you, if you are interested, to be able to start this type of business.

CHAPTER 20: GROWING HEMP IN THE USA

Industrial hemp is the fastest growing crop in American agriculture. The US defines industrial hemp as cannabis sativa plants containing 0.3% or less of THC. Prior to 2015, hemp was virtually non-existent in terms of U.S. agriculture because the Federal Controlled Substances Act prevented it.

Then, in 2014, a new agricultural law opened the industrial cultivation of hemp in experimental form and for pilot programs controlled by the state. The following year, 1,500 acres of hemp were planted in the United States. Today, after hemp was removed from federally controlled substances thanks to the latest Farm Bill of 2018, according to new data from the United States Department of Agriculture (USDA), crops have increased 100 times and have reached 146 thousand acres, about 60 thousand hectares. To make a comparison throughout Europe, 47 thousand hectares were cultivated in 2017.

In 2018 hemp was planted in 18 states and in 2019 that more than doubled, with 37 states growing it for a 350% increase in acreage in December 2018. Leading the way is Montana (over 44,000 acres), which has more than double the area of the second state - Colorado - when it comes to growing hemp.

Meanwhile, the US Department of Agriculture is rolling out a new pilot hemp insurance program, which will provide Actual Production History coverage under the agency's Multi-

Peril Crop Insurance program. The new insurance program comes on top of federal crop insurance, to which the USDA has said hemp growers will have access in August.

In Arizona a specific law to identify the pesticides allowed for the cultivation of cannabis for therapeutic purposes

A panel of the most reputable operators in the cannabis sector has been defined to determine which pesticides can be allowed in the industry of the sector. Any final decision must be approved by the Department of Health Services.

Under a law passed last year in Arizona to test cannabis-derived products before they are displayed in retail outlets, a 12-member panel will determine which chemicals can be used in the industry. Proponents of the bill, however, call the plan akin to "the fox watching the chicken coop" since six of the panel members are representatives of the medical cannabis business, the Arizona Capitol Times reports.

Majority leader Sonny Borrelli (Republican) said he would prefer an outright ban on certain chemicals rather than leave it all to the panel which, in addition to six industry members, includes the owner of an Arizona-based cannabis testing lab, an assistant, a caregiver, a laboratory scientist, a health care provider, and a representative of the State Department of Public Safety.

Borrelli has set his sights on the Eagle 20 fungicide, which has been defined as banned on tobacco and a 'heavy carcinogen' but is allowed to be used for growing cannabis in the state under the current regime.

Borrelli introduced a bill that would specifically ban the use of any pesticides except those that the Federal Insecticide, Fungicide and Rodenticide Act claim are benign and require no regulation at all: castor oil, cinnamon oil, garlic, lemongrass oil, rosemary, sesame and white pepper.

"Suppose the card we put together this year shows up and says, Well, are you allowed to use Eagle 20 (in) a certain amount? Antifungal pesticides are needed because all these growth structures are indoors. So they want to be able to mitigate the mold that is found on marijuana," Borrelli told the Capitol Times.

Pele Peacock Fischer, lobbyist for the Arizona Dispensaries Association, said that while the organization is "trying to put together a testing regimen that is extremely safe for patients," it is also trying to find a balance "that you work in the industry so that laboratories can meet demand, [and] that dispensaries can implement". Additionally, Fischer said even if the panel does approve a pesticide that could be potentially harmful, the Department of Health Services has the final say in what is or is not approved.

CHAPTER 21: INCOME FROM CULTIVATION

The food, beverage and bakery products industry is constantly looking for new ingredients and preparations of a vegetable nature, rich in active ingredients with a strong innovative and functional value.

Among the requirements of industry, above all, is safety for humans and animals, which, in other words means:

- absence of heavy metals and contaminants (in general, agricultural land contains many that are absorbed by plants);
- cultivation without pesticides, herbicides, pesticides;
- without aflatoxins;
- without gram negative microorganisms, molds, fungi.

To avoid soil contamination, it must be removed. To eliminate soil, there are two solutions: Hydroponics which contains substrate, and aeroponics without any substrate: the roots are suspended in the air.

Aeroponics is the most advantageous technique, as it is possible, thanks to the apparatus, to customize the vegetable product, increase yields, vary the aromatic character and the active ingredients present in the vegetable biomass and in the flowers. In other words, it is possible to enrich the flower and fortify it with active ingredients to prevent pathologies or fortify diets.

Among the medicinal plants with the highest added value there is hemp with low THC content and about 400 bioactive substances. The plant produces flowers which, like saffron and truffles, are sold by the gram.

A factory of 1026 square meters of aeroponic technology cultivation, in a controlled environment (CEA), aseptic greenhouse in polycarbonate and premises of 196 square meters for processing, employs 6 employees and an annual yield of over 2300 kg distributed in 4 cycles per year.

The flower biomass as it is (without processing) can be sold for 2.5 euros per gram on the wholesale market. The average price is € 5 per gram.

With less than 200 ml of cannabis oil one liter of water, a soft drink can be enriched and help the consumer to sleep well at night.

In this regard, we have built a business plan that takes into account everything that is happening globally, the uses, the problems it solves, the profits it can generate.

What are the profits?

This amounts to millions of euros in the space of a year.

Through aeroponic technology it is possible to obtain 150 grams of dry inflorescence from a single cannabis plant compared to 50 grams of traditional cultivation. The proposed structure, in an aseptic environment, in a greenhouse with natural ventilation, (patented) hosts from a minimum of 3900 plants to a maximum of 6 thousand every 3 months. The germination of seeds is planned in the technical rooms.

Growing legal or light or low-THC cannabis plants, with an aeroponic system, speeds up growth times and increases yields by at least 10% compared to hydroponics and 150% compared to the open field, as well as reducing water inputs, fertilizers, substrates, manpower, the risk of diseases and mold due to excess water, without residues.

The production cycles are distributed 4 times a year, with low plants and adoption of fertilisation techniques aimed at exclusively enlarging the inflorescences with the desired aroma.

This is an innovative cultivation that can be financed by the start & smart measure (with 70 percent mortgage interest-free) or by crowdfunding or through the measures of the 2014-2020 RDP: sub- measures 6.1, 4.1, 4.2.

Or create an operating group and start a test with sub-measure 16.2.

We have prepared a fairly complete version for those who want to diligently investigate the opportunity to grow legal cannabis and maybe someday, when legalized, medical and recreational cannabis.

It is necessary to hurry up, to start experimenting, to start entering the market. The Germans assessed the sector and decided to take the lead in Europe.

You can find online a business plan designed for students, which contains:

1) The document, in addition to the calculation of the individual investment items and related costs, contains a comparison between the yields of the major international players and our system. Well, despite having fixed a lower yield per square meter, our project remains sustainable.

2) I propose the project for a collaboration, to marketing managers or decision makers of the agri-food and cosmetics sector in order to develop new products with cannabis flowers (chocolate bars, fruit juices, enriched bread, enriched breadstick, enriched flours, ice cream, etc).

3) The system is scalable and flexible (cultivation of other medicinal products or baby leaves destined for the IV range market in the event of a market crisis).

4) The system implements product sterilization innovations and the cultivation and processing environments and related equipment (Sterilization from hospital operating room)

Made in the USA
Las Vegas, NV
29 October 2022

58354343R00098